SONGS OF MYSELF: QUARTET

POEMS

Kraftgriots

Also in the series (POETRY)

David Cook *et al*: *Rising Voices*
Olu Oguibe: *A Gathering Fear;* winner, 1992 All Africa Okigbo Prize for Literature & Honourable mention, 1993 Noma Award for Publishing in Africa
Nnimmo Bassey: *Patriots and Cockroaches*
Okinba Launko: *Dream-Seeker on Divining Chain*
Onookome Okome: *Pendants,* winner, 1993 ANA/Cadbury poetry prize
Nnimmo Bassey: *Poems on the Run*
Ebereonwu: *Suddenly God was Naked*
Tunde Olusunle: *Fingermarks*
Joe Ushie: *Lambs at the Shrine*
Chinyere Okafor: *From Earth's Bedchamber*
Ezenwa-Ohaeto: *The Voice of the Night Masquerade,* joint-winner, 1997 ANA, Cadbury poetry prize
George Ehusani: *Fragments of Truth*
Remi Raji: *A Harvest of Laughters,* joint-winner 1997 ANA/Cadbury poetry prize
Patrick Ebewo: *Self-Portrait & Other Poems*
George Ehusani: *Petals of Truth*
Nnimmo Bassey: *Intercepted*
Joe Ushie: *Eclipse in Rwanda*
Femi Oyebode: *Selected Poems*
Ogaga Ifowodo: *Homeland & Other Poems,* winner, 1993 ANA poetry prize
Godwin Uyi Ojo: *Forlorn Dreams*
Tanure Ojaide: *Delta Blues and Home Songs*
Niyi Osundare: *The Word is an Egg* (2000)
Tayo Olafioye: *A Carnival of Looters* (2000)
Ibiwari Ikiriko: *Oily Tears of the Delta* (2000)
Arnold Udoka: *I Am the Woman* (2000)
Akinloye Ojo: *In Flight* (2000)
Joe Ushie: *Hill Songs* (2000)
Ebereonwu: *The Insomniac Dragon* (2000)
Deola Fadipe: *I Make Pondripples* (2000)
Remi Raji: *Webs of Remembrance* (2001)
'Tope Omoniyi: *Farting Presidents and Other Poems* (2001)
Tunde Olusunle: *Rhythm of the Mortar* (2001)
Abdullahi Ismaila: *Ellipsis* (2001)
Tayo Olafioye: *The Parliament of Idiots: Tryst of the Sinators* (2002)
Femi Abodunrin: *It Would Take Time: Conversation with Living Ancestors* (2002)
Nnimmo Bassey: *We Thought It Was Oil But It Was Blood* (2002)
Ebi Yeibo: *A Song For Tomorrow and Other Poems* (2003)
Adebayo Lamikanra: *Heart Sounds* (2003)
Ezenwa-Ohaeto: *The Chants of a Minstrel* (2003), winner, 2004 ANA/NDDC poetry prize and joint-winner, 2005 LNG The Nigeria Prize for Literature
Seyi Adigun: *Kalakini: Songs of Many Colours* (2004)

SONGS OF MYSELF: QUARTET

POEMS

Tanure Ojaide

kraftgriots

Published by

Kraft Books Limited

6A Polytechnic Road, Sango, Ibadan
Box 22084, University of Ibadan Post Office
Ibadan, Oyo State, Nigeria
✆ +234 (0)803 348 2474, +234 (0)805 129 1191
E-mail: kraftbooks@yahoo.com;
kraftbookslimited@gmail.com
Website: www.kraftbookslimited.com

First published 2015

ISBN 978–978–918–331–9

= KRAFTGRIOTS =
(A literary imprint of Kraft Books Limited)

First printing, November 2015

For Anne,

for the constant support and companionship over the decades and also the peace that allows my minstrelsy to thrive.

Foreword

Songs of Myself: Quartet is deeply rooted in the indigenous African poetic tradition. The great *udje* poets first composed songs paying tribute to the god of songs, followed by songs of self-exhortation, and then songs mocking themselves before satirizing others. This collection incorporates some of these aspects of the oral poetic genre in its four-part structure. It deals with self-examination and the minstrel's alter-ego as a way of attempting to know himself. So, there is self-mockery that justifies mocking others. The four parts of the collection are: "Pulling the Thread of the Loom," "Songs of Myself," "Songs of the Homeland Warrior," and "Secret Love and Other Poems."

In the first quartet, the poet assumes the persona of an old man who has experienced much over time and shares his experience of life with others. It ends with advice to youths and speaks on how life has to do with multitasking. In the second quartet, the minstrel presents a persona who mocks himself and in doing so tells us about the society he lives in and its penchant for singling out individuals for criticism. Thus, the poet and his society are simultaneously interrogated in their respective roles in private and public spheres. The third quartet, "Songs of the Homeland Warrior," has to do with the poet's Niger Delta experience. While the persona laments ecological and environmental damage and changes, he criticizes not only outsiders that have caused the damage but also his people's representatives. The concluding quartet, "Secret Love and Other Poems," starts with an emblematic poem and goes on to deal with the poet's inner wanderings and thoughts about life. This section also features a variety of poems. The format of the four-part structure affords the poet the opportunity to deal with personal and public experiences in a closely related fashion. These poems have engaged the poet for more than five years.

Tanure Ojaide
Effurun, Delta State, Nigeria/Charlotte, NC, USA.
August 3, 2015

Contents

Dedication 5
Foreword 6

I *Pulling the Thread of the Loom* 13

Gently 14
No hunger 16
The song uplifts the minstrel 18
Questing 20
The worm 22
Remembering St. Nicholas 23
Drops of my blood 25
On my birthday 26
Exile island 28
Skies without birds 31
Lamentation 32
Without these memories 33
What I remember 35
The song breaks out the day 37
Desert dawn 40
Refuge song 43
After reading *King Leopold's Ghost* 45
Masika 47
Medellin testament 49
Effurun market 51
Okpara night 53
More questions 55
Spirit 57
Certainties 59
For youths 60

For the drowned, at Lampedusa 62
The road to Kilifi 64
Jolly abandon 66

II *Songs of Myself* 67

Everything is a metaphor 68
The facts of my love 70
Mother hen 71
Heartbreaks 72
Song of myself 73
He swears by the pen 75
If the poet were the butt of his own songs 77
To the new wordsmiths 78
Gatherer of honey 80
Your cleanliness astounds me 83
Family counselor 85
Wayo man 87
Acquittal 89
Self-defense 91
I am so predictable 93
On the day of no prohibitions 95
Juju dance 97
The emigrant 98
Consolation 100
Ekanigbogbo 102
The new lotus eaters 105
They say my child is ugly like a goat 107
Learning 108

III *Songs of the Homeland Warrior* 111

If those called militants 112
If they had their gods here 113
Can I still call from the River Nun? 114

Don't follow the palm wine tapper's course 116
In the Omoja River 117
Much of the year wet 118
Only in his memory 120
At Eruemukohwarien 121
The zestful river lost its fine fingers 122
The multitude of fish 124
I pass the same roads 126
Come and spend a day with me 128
I had left home with reluctance 129
On whose side is the truth? 130
Maybe they are right 131
If I were to ask my people 132
We dey chop akara dey go 133
So many questions 134
In the theater of war 136
In wake keeping 137
For the wind that still blows 139

IV *Secret Love and Other Poems* 141

The painting suite 142
Secret love 146
In contest 150
For the muse of peace 152
Apprehension 154
We have grown 155
For Ayesiri 157
Pantun suite 159
(Re)visitation 160
Homage: To my friend's father 161
Death of a senator 163
Let them die for Arsenal 165
In a tent room 168
Masks 169

Wrestlers 171
Of humidity and hydration 173
Next to God 176
Waiting 177
For the New Year 178

I

Pulling the Thread of the Loom

Gently and steadily the old man pulls the thread of the loom.

Gently

*Dede-e dede-e**

Gently and steadily the old man pulls the thread of the loom.

Dede-e dede-e

He limps his way through the rugged terrain that stretches before him
but outpaces strides of those without age or other kinds of challenges.

Dede-e dede-e

The cotton tree stands unnoticed amidst iroko and palm trees
but its soft sheets of fabric cover the entire world's nakedness.

Dede-e dede-e

It's not only years that confer wisdom, says the young crocodile
that has dug its hole with tools of its mouth and satiated with fish.

Dede-e dede-e

It's not the hulk that gives one power, boasts the black ant after
stabbing the elephant's butt and downing the giant of the jungle.

Dede-e dede-e

One's speed comes not just from a multiplicity of limbs,
the two-legged mocks the millipede it always flashes past.

Dede-e dede-e

More than thrice, and accompanied by its kind, the cock crows at dawn
but only once does the cheerful but taciturn sun rise to wake up the world.

Dede-e dede-e

I am not a priest but consecrated a temple on the mountain's top
where I chant invocations and panegyrics to my benevolent muse.

Dede-e dede-e

Nor am I a king with the paraphernalia that weighs down the unwary
but I am covered with songs assuaging every ache that afflicts the head.

Dede-e dede-e

Gently and steadily the old man pulls the thread of the loom.

Dede-e dede-e.

- *Dede-e dede-e*: onomatopoeic expression of "gently" in the Urhobo language.

No hunger

"I have no hunger in the famine of words" (Remi Raji)

The minstrel suffers no hunger
in the famine of songs

since his muse always provides
from the divine abundance.

Aridon's favorite suffers no hunger
in the famine of songs;

his eyes rest on every beauty
he discovers and sings about

and even the aches he suffers
resonate in a rhythmic cry.

The muse's favorite suffers no hunger
in the famine of songs—

the cotton tree's worm suffers no nakedness
in the famine of fabrics,

and opulent thrives its wardrobe
even as the rest of the world wears tatters.

The minstrel suffers no hunger
in the famine of songs—

lavished the minstrel's love,
the muse is so happy

the fortunate traveler meets no peril
even when the road waits famished.

The muse bubbling with zest
and ever so beautiful,

the minstrel remains filled
in the famine of love.

The god of songs suffers no hunger
in the famine of ardent worshipers—

for sure the minstrel suffers no hunger
in the famine of songs.

• Aridon: god of memory and song/poetry among the Urhobo people.

The song uplifts the minstrel

Water empowers the crocodile
the song uplifts the minstrel

the sun smiles its way across the earth
the full moon smothers night with a silvery sheet

water empowers the crocodile
the song uplifts the minstrel

love intoxicates partners with a joyful heart
rain showers farmers with hope of a plentiful harvest

water empowers the crocodile
the song uplifts the minstrel

the wind fans harmattan flames with pagan flourish
the peacock enthralls with a fanfare of rainbow colors

water empowers the crocodile
the song uplifts the minstrel

the proverb spices the tongue with sparkling delight
the cherry tree lavishes the ripest fruits on its favorites

water empowers the crocodile
the song uplifts the minstrel

the eagle on the iroko stretches vision
the crow cuts straight to its destination

water empowers the crocodile
the song uplifts the minstrel

dawn gingerly accelerates the early traveler's steps
flight compels distance to perform a disappearing act

water empowers the crocodile
the song uplifts the minstrel

the wind blows and the wiregrass dances
tireless the possessed dancer in a torrent of music

water empowers the crocodile
the song uplifts the minstrel

from right, left, and other sides the market fills up
from hard rock the spring dispenses fresh draughts

water empowers the crocodile
the song uplifts the minstrel

mounting one another rice cooks and fills the pot
one womb alone procreates a vast clan of kinsfolks

water empowers the crocodile
the song always uplifts the minstrel.

Questing

I come to you, *Evwerhe Amre**, far-sighted deity,
you who lead the quester to find what he seeks.

With a folder of petitions that I want answered,
I have carried it from start to be settled someday:

I seek love to land at the bosom of my favorite
but get distracted by sirens out to frustrate me;

I want to hold hands, laugh hilariously relishing
sweet berries but continue on a lonesome road

and all I have found in sixty years of seeking
hugging a divine beauty only in daydreams.

I seek the iroko king of trees to proliferate
but the entire species barely survives poachers;

I seek a land swept clean of cleptomaniac leaders
but the population has become a thieving army.

Evwerhe Amre, I come to you deity of success
promising arrival for the journey started

completion of the task embarked upon;
reward for what I pray and work for.

How many full moons have I waited to share
the hallowed disk with a farming queen,

how many floods have I sought Mami Wata
to surrender her horny self to my serenades;

how many decades continue to seek the laurel
you promised me in the singing caste?

I seek to find what my head can carry without
crushing the coconut shell harboring my brains;

I seek what will fill my heart with exhilaration
and strength without fear of suffering failure.

Great deity of Orhoakpor,* give me the capacity
to hold tenaciously onto what you lead me to find:

the love so down-to-earth no wind can shake it;
the friendship that's enduring partnership of love.

---

* *Evwerhe Amre*: deity of seeking and finding; also by implication of success and greatness.

* Orhoakpor: a town in Agbon Kingdom, Ethiope East Local Government in Nigeria's Delta State.

The worm

Despite promises of a fabulous largesse in other industries,
I would rather take to the worm's business on the cotton tree.

With that I know things would never come that low
for me to be left with nothing and go about naked;

I would rather wear a cotton suit in my want,
remain very human even without a cache of cash

and nobody would take me for a madman
flaunting tatters or nudity; a public spectacle.

I would rather take to the task of the worm
and make the cotton tree my residence

than take to politics that's bound to have a down-turn
or teach and later be scorned by those I had mentored.

Nor would I these days be a contractor or a banker
who could crash with a bang with the Stock Market;

I would rather do the bush labor of the worm
whose silk will forever be favored over other fabrics.

I would rather take to the industry of the worm
than seek a skyscraper for a business office,

I would rather be a contented worm always dancing
than take to any other trade that is bound to slump.

Remembering St. Nicholas

(in memory of Joe Ewubare)

Images of St. Nicholas Hospital assault me:
doors opening and closing, gurneys moving
a stream of patients through gray passageways;
oxygen cylinders in tow to keep masks in place
and white and blue jostling between life and death.

At the ICU* resident doctors and nurses sit chatting,
waiting to respond at quick notice to abnormalities
in heartbeat or breathing on the monitors; the graphs
zigzag up and down. Is life a tower that death flattens
as the champion wrestler does to claim a prized trophy?

The images will not go—doctors in white, nurses in white
or blue; patients subsumed in color codes they can't read.
There are colors that make no sense of health or disease;
colors that cannot be diagnosed leaning towards death or life.
St. Nicholas has a hundred rooms draped gray, not white.

And from the ICU to regular rooms gray in outlook,
the tide changes from salt to freshwater and the flux
of vitals registers in sighs at both ends: relief or disbelief
in the invisible tug of war taking place all over the wards—
hope melts into despair or despair loses to victorious hope.

So, there are two thieves on the loose in the wards;
two experienced thieves out there to test their craft
stampeding from the stairs, one confident in gait
and the other tentative in a prayerful poise like one
knowing the limited resources against a superior force.

And my third eye shuts when it should open, shuts light
to the gladiators to decide life or death in the open arena;

one a shadow more physical than what my two eyes saw
in the open wound; the other absent but still present, wary
before two eyes opened without seeing the cunning fighters.

I have only prayed for the tide to go out and return—
the way that takes the fisherman home with his catch—
without seeing where at mid-river the current pauses
from incoming and outgoing waters clashing to part ways.
My third eye fails to see the shadow leering at busy doctors

and spirits displaying an obituary only the keenest eye can read;
they sing hymns to accompany the lone celebrant in his craft
just as the tide that races to the ocean dissolves into a mass
that already features the elements that make life and death one
journey that however long must come to a restful destination.

And now how can I forget doors opening and closing,
antiquated lifts opening and closing to shifts of nurses;
the stairs trafficking up and down friends and relatives
that do not allow the patient rest but give good cover
to the cunning shadow aiming shots at the bedridden.

St. Nicholas, rated topmost, still no defense against
the astral archers, shadow gladiators come to abduct
one not given a chance against them despite high fees
and drugs to turn back the tide from the shadow ocean.
On the bed the body drowned in immeasurable tears.

• ICU: Intensive Care Unit.

Drops of my blood

Every drop of my blood adds years to my life,
every drop saves the pool from drying up.

The lancet pierces the flesh with a click;
so sudden it throws back to days of childhood

when the blade's scarification saved from convulsion.
I am no longer a child that simple seizures can kill;

blessed Grandma chanted prayers to the Creator,
a traditional imam's call in her deep devotion.

Every drop of my blood has always saved me—
the razor blade still scares me for its cuts;

a lancet and a razor blade in the same industry
taking on my fingertips, forehead, thumb, or toe.

I always suffer bruises to forestall severe ailments;
every drop of my blood a benevolent reinforcement.

Today's lancet prick yesterday's razor blade cut
drips the same bright blood anxious for my life;

a sharp cut or prick still leaves no sore on the body,
just a pathway for unguents to enter the bloodstream.

My life's been a continuous rite of drawing out blood
to infuse the soul with vital fortifications for the body—

from childhood I have worn amulets to avert peril:
camphor to counter seizures now a new regimen.

Every drop of my blood gives me ample reprieve
from seizures of childhood and surprise attacks

and when I hear ritualists reduce blood to death
I sing of my drops of blood, sustainer of my life.

On my birthday

On my birthday I see ghosts of colleagues
once strutting Marxist peacocks

out everywhere to create a spectacle
of their plumes, a proletarian costume

still living but dead from the turncoat shame
after suffering the massive stroke of charlatans

who had brandished firebrands at every march
and carried the standard for credulous folks

but soon diverted and fell into the cash-covered
ambush to be stifled silent by the weight of greed.

Unmentionable names nobody wants to hear, no
parent allows children access to their stale rhetoric;

vultures that hover over every corridor of power,
nobody sees them without spitting in revulsion.

These living dead are already buried deeper
than the true dead that are remembered;

they won't ever be ancestors of anybody
but forever remain outcasts of humanity

those scholars arguing in defense of *Aa Ba Cha*,
the half-literate butcher of Abuja;

those griots kissing Ogiso's fungoid feet
and stoking fires of torture in Aso Rock;

those experts who for knockout pay prepared
racks to silence freedom fighters in their midst;

those guards who broke into overflowing coffers
and ruined forever the republic's fortune of oil;

those doctors who volunteered their services
of lethal injection to please a mass murderer—

they are living but condemned to holes
in which they lie buried in infamy.

On my birthday, let me flee further
from the bacchanalia of Asaba,

let me not stop at the debauchery of Abuja
that makes mockery of fifty years of adulthood;

let me not be a heart-beat away from executives,
ritual masters who turn democracy into witchcraft;

let me remain the vagabond walking my way
singing in the streets of love and friendship

and let me be friends with those who shun
the wayward fraternity of the living dead.

On my birthday I take flowers to the dead
whose days are always lit with noble splendor

and shun those living whose unmentionable names
already buried them alive and made them ghosts.

(April 24, 2010)

Exile Island

And here in Amassoma, hundreds of years later,
I come for inspiration for songs not yet sung
to the town whose name excoriates my people's
conscience; I come to research trunks of stumps.
To Amassoma, exile island of helpless forebears,
I come a lugubrious heart for rites of atonement.

Exile island once only imagined, Amassoma still
stands; concrete roads over once muddy waterways.
The dark hole now lit with industry charms more
than cities enjoying budgets squandered in sloth.
Amassoma revives despite the years of rampage—
there's no disease that wipes truth from the earth.

Amassoma has been and remains the exile island—
island where suspects of fabricated crimes were
deported to rot but flourished beyond the pale of justice.
They came not in named canoes, heralded by darkness
or stars and moon that witnessed the perjury of power;
they came as stolen cargoes to a preordained fate.

In the population that trickled into the exile island
all suspects were women trivialized by patriarchy,
the demon of society surviving in different shapes.
The culprit covers the monstrous head with a swath
of sanctimonious customs stolen into the culture;
surely the gendered assault reels of premeditation.

And so from the young ladies were purged witches,
from the voiceless gender the pretty ones who would
not be sluts to chiefly or cash-robed men pronounced
witches; the not-so-pretty but mannered not giving in

got labeled witches and freighted overnight into exile
as inglorious men lived free to perjure with more lies.

Of the accused women, none stood trial to be condemned.
Of the thousands of exiles, flagrant victims of trial by ordeal;
those who failed to qualify for innocence before superstitious
councils running villages with their intimidating phalluses.
Banished, they had no tears to shed in the widening rivers
that took them into exile after secret marriage contracts.

A diaspora of my kinsfolks has grown in Amassoma—
traditions kept of forgotten practices but only of women's
prideful heritage and none of the many men's travesties;
songs no longer sung, proverbs now unknown at home
still kept in the vaults of memory because they forget not
whose innocence was their shield; evil ones lose bearing fast.

Memories of pain guide offspring of exiles in Amassoma
and out of collective shame flourish flowers of new growth.
They tell me they speak Urhobo in Amassoma, but who
now remembers the miscarriage of justice and boat trails
of immeasurable sheets of water that stunned every victim
until rising from night willed tears away from life ahead?

Who still remembers the beauties stigmatized at home
to avenge the refusal of old chiefs' marriage proposals
or dalliance to which virtuous ones would not succumb?
Who remembers the Miss Bayelsa of mixed stock came
from centuries of injustice perpetrated by patriarchs
as guards of virtues they violated without reproach?

Amassoma is not only Wilberforce Island, the booty
of white discoverers transported there by poor porters
whose homeland was renamed for the glory of England;
it is the home of coerced ones who were caught running
through thorns rather than just stand and bow without

sacrificing themselves to truth strangled by leaders.

And so into servitude, concubinage, or marriage shame-
less fathers of old sold the cream of their wives' wombs
to the Izon offering foreigners refuge and damned beliefs
of the evil of beauty they could harness into good fortune.
What marriage without the two families celebrating a union?
There was never courtship to nurse love in strange waters.

May the spirit of my kinswomen, smudged with falsehoods
by patriarchal arrogance, live their afterlives triumphant in
the pardon and reprieve the posthumous song grants the innocent.
Now they speak Urhobo in Wilberforce Island, Izon heartland,
and Amassoma thrives as testimony to the undying legacy
of past lawlessness. Today all need redemption collectively.

For those perjured for speaking back against patriarchs,
for the hordes of ghosts stubborn to death denying guilt
for those beauties, virtuous ones, and lone night boaters
of generations that now flower in the rain-flushed sun
I lead the procession seeking forgiveness for violations.
To the wronged ones, dead or alive, I sing this sad song.

Skies without birds

Call it Nembe*, call it by any other Izon name;
this is surely a ghost town—skies without birds.

Where there are no birds children see no kites
to coast along the skyline, no sunbirds to shoot;

where there are no birds elders see no falcons
to celebrate gleefully the year's constant renewal;

there are no hunters in a land of skies without birds;
nothing to draw attention to the sky's haunting mood.

The priests are deprived of animal sacrifice
to gods that have fled the heavens for exile

and Mami Wata has relocated from there
to refuge in un-endowed areas; poor but clean.

No totem birds grace the state's insignia; no
colorful bird to mount the national air fleet.

How does a country attest to sovereignty without
a bird to affirm it, without symbols of freedom?

There are no birds in Nembe but residents spot
vultures, which itself confirms the deathful state.

Surely, this is Ghost Town by an Izon name;
a land of skies without birds is a ghost town.

---

* Nembe: an island town in Nigeria's Bayelsa State; a major oil industry center.

Lamentation

Can I be the mouth of the earth
to cry out what it suffers

from men and women
that daily trample it as if trash

from avid farmers
that do not hesitate to slash and burn it

from poachers
that behead every tree on its feet

from Shell and others
that disembowel it for oil

from developers
that disfigure it indiscriminately

from those it bears sturdily
but care not if it breaks its back

from a host of others
that shit on its face?

It hurts to witness
all the violations rationalized

even as the earth groans dying
by the minute in dignified silence.

Can I be the mouth of the earth
to cry out what it suffers all the time?

Without these memories

Without the past spectacle of beauties and scarecrows
without landmarks standing behind the current station
without voices echoing from long ago to distract from
loud silences threatening to benumb primed ears
how would I appreciate today's vibrant music or give
Timaya* a graceful nod in my crammed solitary room?

Without the naïve love ditties of adolescence
the letter-writing service to big girls to their boys
flames that flickered and disappeared in darkness
birds that disarmed hunters with knockout feathers
the one-night stand that broke the streak of celibacy
all the rigmaroles of roaming the city without a nest
no song to savor unconsummated but contented love.

Without the fall of Greece the rise of Rome
the tyranny of *Aa Ba Cha* the democracy of *Baba*
the goat-head of ineptitude new electoral reforms
the slapping of the deputy the emergence of a president
the ebb and flow of ocean waters in front of Brass
without those memories history would be a lame horse.

Without those flashes in the receding timescape
without myriad lampposts in the dominion of night
without snatches of music in the doldrums of silence
without the warm embrace in the frostbiting harmattan
without the aroma of bread in the oven for the famished
without the fragrance subsuming the rank smell of rot
without colors colliding over each other in daylight
life around would be the same as death, if not worse.

Without these memories charging in and out
covering and opening up old-time wealth

what poverty would be afflicting me today!
Without those photos to go back to and retouch
without the retinue stampeding for recognition
what loneliness would accompany me all year
to destinations of hope set out for without a roadmap
or return from aborted trips to nowhere in particular
down to earth where I am bound to wonder!

---

* Timaya: famous Nigerian pop singer of Bayelsa State origin.

What I remember

What I remember I have kept safe.
I display the flowers I picked from behind
when in bloom in an auspicious season
that make me forget the bruises of today's briars.

My love has not lost the luster of old
because ageless in her prime I caught her;
my love has remained constant all the years
because of the everlasting moment of fulfillment.

What I remember of love is stored
with fragrance in a garden of blooming bougainvillea;
the passionate compliments a harvest of reminiscences
that crowd the timescape with contentment.

I need no aquamarine to soak the timeless tokens,
need not secure a ring of loyalty in a bank safe;
what I remember I have kept in the open and can't
be robbed and so remains invaluable for all times.

What I transfer from one residence to another
glows with waxing warmth of earth colors;
what I carry from one year to another dissolves
the grey of birthday anniversaries into light.

The token of friendship remains without rust
even if an iron band meant to fuel our lust;
the love declaration retains its cheerful mirth
and becomes the indelible alphabet of joy.

What I remember of the past is the brush
of living colors with which I paint my life,
the keen palate that is the aftertaste of lunch
and dinner and the communion's company.

I sing of the remembrance of things past,
things that festoon today with smiles;
I sing the erasure of darkness and smudges
in the sun that rests perpetually on a calm face.

The song breaks out the day

I saw a vision

the Almighty a bearded patrician doling out
stuff to every prayerful outstretched hand
each person wearing a halo of yellowish hue
the electricity company imposed on the nation
the domestic animals wild and bush ones tamed
with a spell an apprentice hunter cast on them

the road a corporate snake with a smug skin
named after an apostate of democracy
plants stood at attention to welcome drivers
in their sedentary theatrics of serfs to the armed
the land bounced pedestrians as if beneath
generous gods were playing Ping-Pong
to while away the boredom of eternity
and so sought sacrifices from humans
miserly and denying them their divinity

love came from its isolated garden station
to accost its ally friendship in an open house
and it was not clear in the street which was which
and not the other for all the talk and appearances
both rivals that wanted all or nothing of the partner

every day a workday on the fertile hard soil
every night a vacation to replenish industry
of course the day broke on its own terms
without misted eyes that infuriated dawn
without cockcrows turning clocks into sentinels
without the shifts of publicized sinecure jobs,
a burden the Swiss ambassador hastily declined
without the appearance of the sun from its throne

to wave a firebrand like a revolutionary flag
there was no darkness by nightfall to summon
the wearied and married ones to their beds

there was no death for the sick in the ICU
where each patient saw two worlds cohabiting
with a shadow looking different from the body
every life wore a bright cloud and knew not
that time passed like a thief eyeing the body
to be taking chunks piecemeal for its supper
to which no sensible person was invited
so as to draw an invisible line for the unwary
to cross and transform into a ghost of the future

the women were birds of flaming plumes
everywhere seeking nectar from lewd flowers
and gave the earth a beauty that lulls
the dynasty of tyrants to abdicate the throne
with prayers for deliverance
the men took freedom for granted and denied
others not parading the phallus as a standard
as no men but women on whose heads they sat
to drink palm wine and eat delicacies served them
until they lost their virility and were laughed out

the veteran swimmers all drowned at knee depths
and were hailed for their choice of martyrdom
since nobody wanted suicide by another name
the color red was no show in the rainbow that
had it missing from the peacock assembly
the desert air of Gashua* was a sea breeze
and the beaches of Brass wore on their faces
the designer powder of a sophisticated seductress
that brought waves from Mami Wata's coral palace
because she was horny and wanted a partner
she couldn't get and so fell into delirious tantrums

the song came from stones a melody of machines
tears from quarries since blood's in short supply
in emergency rooms across the republic of love
and all the rocky mountains breasts of the earth
the hills and valleys sang Papa Wemba's Lingala tunes*
and nodding feverishly in the open-air concert
that so possessed the minstrel to testify to the magic
of polyrhythmic music that fed the imagination

the day the poem comes, it comes simply dressed
so as not to be seen and mobbed before its outing
or marked for assassination by rivals, politicians
the bride holds the lamp over masquerades
who are really drummers for the great dance

poetry comes the day I am intoxicated without drinking
I am up despite being knocked down by love fever
I stare with wonder at the possibility of capturing
the warrior brigade of superpower arrogance
releasing from incarceration the fish in the Volta Lake
a newborn's cries despite Warri's curfew hours
and the mobile police trigger-ready to shoot at voices
the ocean waves lifting a row boat and hanging it
on the mangrove standing ready to save from drowning.

---

* Gashua: a town in Yobe State in the Sahel region of Nigeria.
* Papa Wemba: Congolese musician who sings in Lingala.

Desert dawn

In the millennial decade of its existence
carrying faith as a heavy but necessary standard

the desert lost its vast emptiness of dust and dunes
to millions of plants springing up in town and bush.

Folks used to fearing storms as evil spirits on the loose
ripping landscapes littering death and debris

but this storm is a resurgence of will, a raging
explosion of "No!" to legendary tears and losses.

And so carrying faith a steel talisman against tyranny
the desert springs forth millions of trees in town and bush,

and the sand the desert's underling can no longer be trampled upon
but stands a forest of shades in numbers no Pharaoh can cut down

with an army of orders that desecrate the purity of the Book
calling for disobedience and elimination of straying leaders.

Millions of plants spring up to cover town and bush
where once only sand and dust were the blind guards.

Call it a spring's awakening, a novel season
and they throw stones not as the pilgrims' last rite

but at hardened clay gods they had worshiped
for so long in ignorance and fear of shadows;

they had shed blood without complaint;
they had suffered incarceration in silence

and almost came to believe that self-immolation
for the devil's cohort was an act of the Almighty.

But they suddenly realized clay dissolves in a storm;
a mold the devil put there to scare hell out of them

into submission to dissolute practices that twist
the straight lives bequeathed to them from above.

At dawn they realized they could execute gods
that did not live to godly behavior and deeds;

they could down idols and drag them in the street
and bury them in forlorn sand dunes of mass contempt;

they would rather bury gods allied to evil djinns
than robe them with glamour of their stolen wealth.

The desert is awash with this millennial storm;
millions of trees flaunting green over the vastness.

At dawn the desert cannot be silenced from liberating
itself from the dynastic savagery of successive sun gods;

the desert landscape wears a terrible armor
in the battle against apostates of faith, sphinxes.

The desert wakes from the deep night of compliance
to self-sacrifice to hardened clay gods of the soil

that thrived on blood and sweat of servers
without reciprocating the sacrifice of patriots.

For long I looked northward and laughed
at the desert culture of affluence of dust,

saw the bonfire of divine-proffered wealth
that a few ordained themselves as kings to burn.

All these years I have spent time and energy
preaching against desert encroachment

and sang the tale of the harmattan to listeners
whose ears had gone numb from cold dust winds,

but now I wish the desert storm of the spring's dawn
to sweep through my indolent forest, shake millions

and blow them out of the refuge of anomic existence
into town and bush filled with millions of up-thrust fists.

Refuge song

A crowd crying for relentless attention assaults my memory
seeking refuge in my song that prepares to take in even more:

women whose arresting beauty I could not acknowledge before them,
hallucinating flowers I couldn't pluck away without accusation of theft;

wives and widows that patriarchs put to sacrifice on top of their men,
orphans condemned without trial for crimes they did not commit.

I keep robbers of plantation owners free in the open house of my song,
honor prostitutes unlike those who call them names but sell themselves.

In the city of rednecks hounded black men have private rooms in the song;
in the street of evangelicals the song opens its doors to confessed secularists.

Rainforest trees escaping poaching developers flourish in the bio-diverse song,
indigenous peoples pressed to abandon their ways win court cases in the song;

all those targeted for ethnic cleansing take the Underground Railroad to my song,
the minstrel leads ghosts of extinct animals to their revived habitats in the song

as the vanished herbs of indigenous knowledge grow luxuriant in my song
and the proverbs of primeval languages spirited into the safety of the song.

I don't mind those who say I harbor criminals in the outhouse of my song
but who mask their capital crimes in meek Sunday-churchgoing habits

nor those who say I live with deviants of free folks in my house of words
but are so depraved you wonder if they have any human tissues in them.

I want all peoples of the world to gather for a party in my song
so that color, race, and other nonsensical tags will be trashed.

I give cover in the song to millions under fire from all directions
and will lead them through the hazards to their safe destinations—

the large army I have mobilized under cover of singing
can break any siege meant to crack the strongest backbone;

this crowd of rejuvenated survivors in the republic of my song
marches on serenading the refuge we all defend in my memory.

After reading *King Leopold's Ghost*

> "Forgetting one's participation in mass murder is not something passive; it is an active deed." (Adam Hochschild)

1

Memory reels backward the landscape
of murderers on the loose

and the scars open up the savage wounds
that won't go with the millennial passage.

My kinsfolks wanted to die rather than live
under the scourge of Godless strangers;

they would rather die than be shot at for sport
or crushed for ivory and rubber to enrich others.

And so history marches on, awarding Stanley and
Leopold as Mobutu medals of ultimate dishonor!

2

All the profits from ivory and rubber
that maimed or killed hundreds of thousands

the old king threw into procuring dresses
for a teenage prostitute as a royal paramour.

See the scoundrel brandishing a humanitarian flag
while *chicotte**-whipping and shackling farmers

and decking streets of Brussels with arches of ivory
to the applause of admirers of his mass murdering!

A convulsive dance of death for Caroline razes
Congo in a hurricane of apocryphal magnitude:

all the severed hands and cracked skulls, all the tears
of wood and folks for the love of a teenage prostitute!

---

* *chicotte*: a leather strip that inflicted biting pain when used to flog a person. It was a notorious tool used to torture the Congolese people for ivory and rubber in King Leopold's Congo.

Masika*

(for rape victims of Congo DR)

Watching the Aljazeera special, a painful
wound; the body's nerves torn into shreds.

This is not what tears alone will cure
since one can drown in self-raised deluge;

hence laughter to bury the sordid act
and rise above it all to heal and live.

In the group marching with choral songs
to the field, deciding to mend their world

rather than suicide for not only violation
by brutes wearing the mask of humanity

but also collective rejection by family,
friends, and neighbors; haunted outcasts.

Do you take your life after escaping mauling;
do for marauders what they failed to achieve?

Wounds, however deep, Masika teaches,
surely heal with persistent nursing and love.

To you Masika, mother of broken women
and their tainted children, my air-thrust fist!

You bring to life those destroyed
in the terrible war and home fronts;

you rid the world of evil taints and tears
and brush fresh the bitter-smacked mouth—

a miracle only in the purview of prophets
you perform with songs and zest for new life.

---

* Masika: woman who takes in raped victims and their children shunned by relatives and friends in Congo DR and organizes group farming as therapy.

Medellin testament

1. Of Bolivar* and Liberation

It's not surprising that in marble Bolivar stands
tall in the market-center beside the cathedral.
Along the street pastry shops whose aroma
tempts me to break the fast that's not yet due.
But in the market, steps of the cathedral,
and adjoining streets sprawls a destitute army
sitting disheveled or lying down as if lifeless.
For what was the liberation to these beggars?

In the nearby park, baseball capped seniors
in T-shirts exercising and walking past misery.
Facing the park again another gothic church
and in marble heroes, poets, and the Virgin Mary;
a past in which every heart beat with contentment.
In the early Saturday morning young ones out—
life flows all forms of detritus and disruptions.
Here in Medellin I have not heard of Escobar,
nor the rusty guns of FARC in the forest.

2. At the Museo Antioquia

At the Antioquia Museum, Botero's voluminous
women and figures that define him Colombian.
Some other artist paints *Bandit Woman* black
to perjure the voiceless and still get paid for it.
Another paints a sweet black child, fruits on her lap,
as if to fend off hunger that's poaching her kinsfolks.

Bolivar stands tall after liberating half a continent
with men trained in Haiti for the revolution.
The Haitian host, asked for recompense, simply said:

"Don't mention my name!" Of course, Bolivar felt
such goodness should not be buried in the chest.
For history to tell the truth, he proclaimed the name!

---

* Bolivar (1783—1830): liberator of Colombia, Venezuela, Ecuador, and Peru.

Effurun market

By the dreaded Egba* Shrine we dared not get close to,
by the space ceded to powers alive and dead and feared

by the sacred ground of all days the market gathers
from every direction known to humans; they press in

a traffic that only spirits can control but not *Yellow Fever**.
They throng in, children, men, and women, some pregnant.

Spirits and humans comingle in this mass every eight days;
every eight days there's no lie to this market-day to which

known and unknown merchants come with magic wares
and no-one dares bring in spirits to play human pranks—

so no market-day can be re-scheduled for another day;
no calamity postpones the market, the day of no burials.

On this day we are devotees of Egba who must be cheered
by the crowd assembled in his shadow to entertain him

with the subterfuges of traders and buyers—all tortoises
shaking hands with closed fists, seeking an upper hand.

On this day we flow along the human press that's more of
the spirit world of fairytales that we live without knowing.

The warrior god guards those doing transactions, bartering off
what's not dear to them but pricing it as if so invaluable;

the trader and the buyer share the same philosophy
of keeping much of theirs and still getting from others!

Is Egba just on sentry duty overseeing the grounds
and laughing at the animals calling themselves humans

trying hard to outsmart each other in the pricing game;
laughing loud while backbiting those they are helping?

Believers of every faith with contradictory creeds gather here
to shower the deity with glory denied him on Sunday pulpits—

who forbids foodstuffs from the market and still lives; who
lives without the grace of the market-god, the food manager?

I come to mingle with spirits of the living and the dead,
I come to mingle with strangers, the aliases of spirits.

I come to see secret lovers have their day under cover
of pressing buyers and sellers and speak heart to heart;

they have their day amidst the eternal bustle of the market;
they smile lavishly amidst spices of all colors and aromas.

On this Effurun market-day I come to see what goes on
besides buying and selling.This surely isn't Sarmakand!

---

* Egba: god of war of the Uvwie people of Effurun in Delta State, Nigeria.
* *Yellow Fever*: local traffic wardens dressed in yellow uniform.

Okpara night

1

In the serene silence thoughts morph
into more than a thousand and one shapes—

not even a hiss of the resplendent stars
to accentuate the cat's walk into sound;

no breath upsets the elevated poise of the stars,
this dark no song articulates this harmony.

Life here thrives in a quiet pulse that
has a healthy equilibrium of its own.

I hear no song, no breath, no cries; only
words thought out morph into pictures

populating the dark with more than a thousand
and one lives corresponding in serene silence;

the imagined spectacle of my muse asleep
peaceful for once before jealous tantrums.

I am at peace not to execute tasks to the letter
since the world is at peace with its own troubles;

no master no servant only silence of the stars
that overhead watch over all heavy as rocks.

On this silent night thoughts morph into more
than a thousand and one times into still images,

masterpiece subjects that can only be imagined
than experienced in daylight; so divinely blessed.

2

In this vastness life thrives in dark silences,
the aurora flashes wordless colors of beauty.

Silence is not deaf to the ditties of the mind;
the wind lives on the divine breath of spirits

nor silence blind to blooming pageants,
ears and eyes bonded in surreal complicity.

Silence knows how to impel a stream
in slow motion into a still ocean of life

as the choral pause of pre-dawn orchestra
holds me spellbound, suspended in silence.

When there's no motion thoughts fly high;
everything swathed in darkness and shadows

there's nothing to hold to in the emptiness,
more than a thousand and one in silent refuge

under cover of human rights and freedom.
I hold firmly to the large wings of silence

for a craft that transports all in still pose.
I am a guest in the silent republic of night

waiting for dawn and its ritual stampede
for notes that will spring out of nothing.

I am ensconced in the down of silence
parading thoughts of approaching dawn.

More questions

1

There are more questions now than before to answer;
paucity of answers to harder questions asked.

A sixty-year-old well cannot douse the flames
fuelled by the instant resurgence of old memories;

after sixty years the destination gets more distant as
the horizon leers at the sage searching for every answer.

How does the guard know that the fugitive banging at the gate
isn't a robber coming in to assault hospitality with a shotgun?

How does the bird respond to the tortoise it flew to riches
only to be left unrequited, a laughingstock of the trickster?

What does the driver tell the jury he constitutes in his heart
after discovering he has given a convict a ride to freedom?

I wear scars that do not prevent further wounds in the thorn bush;
the road walked for decades now a steeper hill and a lower valley.

There are more questions now than before to answer,
paucity of answers to harder questions asked.

2

I hear reports from two contesting sides and know
not which to believe in the gossip frenzy of the day.

Each swears telling me the truth in confidence
but I know that both are lying to score points—

there can be only one truth and it cannot be otherwise;
lies know how to wear diverse costumes to impress.

Only my ears, forced into this courthouse where they must
hear what different advocates will plead to be credible,

suffer the indignity of being insulted as dumb fellows
when in fact they know the truth that is in neither lies.

Spirit

(for Chimalum Nwankwo)

Spirit of Anambra, you are spirit everywhere
your spirit my spirit a life of stubborn roots

why are we not spirit of Nigeria
choked by rank smell

and claiming permanent residence
of a land we despise as not ours?

Spirit of Nigeria on the loose abroad
seeking return to embrace peace

despite bombs ripping bodies
and the suffocating stink of the land!

Spirit of the dead, spirit of the living
a masquerade flogging onlookers in the arena

for the secrets they hide in their closets
secrets so pallid they must be hidden

and closets so huge they can accommodate
mortal sins that do not kill ardent criminals;

secrets they hide in their groins or breasts
of which silence is the supreme guardian.

Spirit, we first met at the crossroads of America
where every direction leads to perdition

since no belief in the wandering spirit she mocks
but only on wheels of fortune spinning so fast.

Spirit of succor, spirit of courage, spirit of desires
we sit or stand on breakable tools and do not crash;

we follow the water queen without canoe and not drown,
we execute corrupt fathers-in-law to fuel our love.

I realize your mother conceived after gathering your spirit
into her basket at the *udala* tree on a blazing moonlit night

and only Spirit will converse with his 90-year-old mother
in a mansion of countless rooms dampened by diaspora shadows.

If you were not Spirit those Gwodogwodo mercenaries
would have brought you down in the battlefield

but no artillery fire however sustained threatens Spirit;
no bombardment comes to the invisible spot of Spirit!

Spirit of the living mischief-maker in the dark
your wine rack rivals Ogun's gourds at festival time

you are spirit of everybody human seeking love
that awakens and rejuvenates body, mind and spirit!

Ndimuo! Ndimuo! Ndimuo!
It's the spirit that leads one in life.

Spirit of the living clothes us.
Ndimuo! Ndimuo! Ndimuo!

Certainties

If I lived a thousand years ago in the future,
I would be a desecrated god out of fashion
broken into pieces and mended into a figure
at once dead and still living free and sound
in the legendary vault of a disillusioned present.

The wretches and life-wrecked of today just
fallen gods; the lords of tomorrow not contemplated
in the hordes roaming the streets as miscreants
preparing for the inevitable metamorphoses
that will eventually make life eternal for all.

I have lived in rooms of mansions not yet built
in the open lots created out of impending chaos;
I am heading inexorably for crossroads of highways
that know nothing of spirits and sacrifice.
And yet I am a popular name forgotten before birth.

I am filing documents encrypted in non-existent
alphabets, throwing dust to powder the wind's face.
After all the uploads and downloads of lives,
where are the certainties to count on or contend with
as the refuge from inanities, the calm from chaos?

Others are coming that were gone before;
we are the belated ancestors of millennia.
The new fruits no longer have the taste
of the past, and there will be no life for the living;
no death for the dead; only unending incarnations.

For youths

Omo Okogbe
Okogbe

Omo Okogbe
Okogbe

He entered with the gait of one spoiling for a fight.
He came in wearing charms on his arms and feet.

Omo Okogbe
Okogbe

He shouted down everyone he came to meet at the gathering.
He had no patience for anybody wearing charms as he did.

Omo Okogbe
Okogbe

Nobody knew where he came from, not to talk of his name.
Nobody remembered his grandfather had been a warrior chief.

Omo Okogbe
Okogbe

Who cared whether he was a messenger from a commander?
He did not bring the pride of whoever sent him to this place.

Omo Okogbe
Okogbe

So he hastily took on the kind of fight he had never trained for.
It took no time to settle his status on the arena—he lost his life.

Omo Okogbe
Okogbe

Now a song mocks the youth rushing in to challenge
those already out in the field or coming in with tight lips:

Omo Okogbe
Okogbe

Omo Okogbe
Okogbe

For the drowned, at Lampedusa

Without visas the martyrs of hope tunnel
the Sahara to the Mediterranean cemetery.

I hear their prayers in the pastors' sermons;
those who pray for miracles but still drown—

no parents at home aware of the hapless flight
shed tears for the high hope broken by waves.

The morning call wakes the street before dawn
to transmit a message of salvation in deep waters.

Damn your fears and fly to seize your destined life;
there's no sea the swallow cannot overfly at heart

and the bell rings to awaken those still dreaming
before day draws the ears of the all-night vigil!

But where will you live without terra firma since
Europe's air and water don't yield to African prayers?

The seabed waits for migrants in their rickety boats,
beckons them to arrive there and meet no protests!

At home the intercessors are on sore knees ferrying
alive boatloads of youths to their inland destinations;

nobody wants to stay safe suffering hardship
but boats topple for Lampedusa to supply caskets.

They tunnel the Sahara and absorb the vast oven
but cannot cross the blue-eyed sea, charming blonde

standing between them and the shining city ahead;
behind shanties abandoned forever for better or worse

they suffer sandstorms that make night of day
but capitulate body and soul to the marine spirit.

On Sunday the sermons call for faith to walk on
water as Jesus did but nobody weeps as Jesus wept

the parents expecting Western Union in months
unaware of the sea's harvest of their sustaining crops

unaware of the grave loss their loins have suffered
and suspended in hope for the rest of their lifetimes.

How do we bring home what we seek from afar
without movement encountering sand and water,

how tunnel the Sahara swallowing the big bone
to Europe without drowning at its very doorstep?

The road to Kilifi

On the bus from Nairobi to Kilifi*
Africa's fate rolls like a dice.

We could be victims of outsiders
who see us different in faith

as well as victims of ourselves
knowing our vulnerability as profit;

it's such a terrible beauty
of giraffes, lions, and gazelles.

I fall in love with the landscape
but fear what feeds on it—

roaming carnivores and zealots;
none saner than the other.

Really I fear no lions but cross-
border raids by mad faith-fools

who would shed blood in place of
Umoja, shoot their way into my heart.

I am safer at the steel fangs of the lion
trained to cavort with strangers

than before professors of faith;
short-fused sectarians, detonators.

The big bus moves, a steel animal
on a smooth tarmac road;

the throttle drowns the silence
as eerie music assaults ears.

Beauty is not safe from mauling.
I seek no martyrdom on the road to Kilifi.

So many memories assault me
not to forget the beauty I have seen

and yet so imperiled; the sun rising
amidst wishes of Umoja and Jambo.

Africa's fate rolls like a dice
on this road from Nairobi to Kilifi.

---

* Kilifi: coastal town in northeastern Kenya.

Jolly abandon

For days dark or lit
I digest voraciously
what a cousin uttered so casually
he no doubt immediately forgot

in the early evening breeze of Effurun
before generators started to cough out fumes
and confuse the star-festooned sky with fury.
The beautifully-pointed words hit me gently:

We chew savory roasted corn
with the season's jolly abandon
even as we weave intently
the intricate fishing net.

I sing a song from the tattered notes of verbiage,
mine diamond in an abandoned muddy landscape;
I pick what pathfinders left behind or discarded
to lighten the burden that threatened their sanity.

Now I carry what's light to lift from the ground
yet crushing on the head but which others envy.
I tap palm wine from the forest in my backyard;
bountiful beauty out of daily self-raised silence.

On and on we go crafting
the intricate weave of the fishing net
as we exchange boisterous banter
with fellow fishers and visiting friends.

We chew savory roasted corn
with the season's jolly abandon
even as we weave intently
the intricate fishing net.

II

Songs of Myself

. . . even the brave fear a battle!

Everything is a metaphor

Everything is a metaphor
the child's chattering laughter

the elder's restrained flood of tears
forever bickering man and woman

everything is a metaphor
the tortoise's silent fart

the lost tail of the leopard
full breasts of a beauty

everything is a metaphor
death on a birthday

a cow and a flea one journey
a lion and a deer one savannah

everything is a metaphor
a woman in a council of men

a man dancing the mother-mask
a queen flaunting a warrior's phallus

everything is a metaphor
tears of laughter

pricks of pleasure
dying to live

everything is a metaphor
a dumb bell

the vision of naught
the voice of silence

everything is a metaphor
ghost of the living

the sun entombed in night
illumination of the blind

everything is a metaphor
the absent but present

hidden in the open
cleansing with mud

everything is a metaphor
life is a tree

a tree an animal
an animal dirt

dirt nurtures life
life sustains death

to the minstrel
everything is a metaphor.

The facts of my love

The facts of my love will unsettle my people:

she pushed out her father to drown to save me in a dugout for two
she assassinated her brother who swore I couldn't marry her sister

because we want nobody to see us as lovers in the intolerant town
we meet in the forest of ghommids beyond the pale of human eyes

there we swathe ourselves in an interminable sheet of green entangled
there we breathe moist air the rains proffer on us under leafy canopies

but in town she can't be mine and the masks we wear no guarantee
that street hordes will not wield machetes and guns against us together

I know the intimidating spirits can no longer keep her away with fear
she loves me the most because she doesn't want to leave me but has to

my people will easily pass judgment on her behavior if they see us together
and they will bind her to the shrine of their rightwing ancestors and gods—

to us the ancestors are dead and have no power to watch from anywhere
the gods lost their divinity when they could not defend their devotees

those scared of women's inevitable revolt take up arms to defend manhood
those who want to keep the outmoded system of chattel slavery are mobilizing

they will not want a modern revolution to sweep their dirt out of the land
they even fear to lose what makes them stupid before the rest of the world

they say we turn upside down what they have kept upright for ages
they say we take a different albeit free road they cannot walk through

surely the facts of our love will unsettle our people.

Mother hen

My muse is a mother hen with a large brood;

there's no way of reaching her in the fragile ecology
of the place without stepping on any of the young ones.

She forages everywhere for food, tenderly picks morsel
after morsel to deposit with a love song at each chick's beak;

she eats little or nothing until after filling all the chicks.
She has no desires to satisfy other than those of her brood;

she cannot fly straight when summoned in an emergency,
she's always running after one chick or the other in the yard.

My muse is a mother hen sitting expansively over her chicks;
she covers them with flaring feathers and pugnacious eyes.

She would sit sleepless on the roof of anywhere her chicks slept;
she glances furtively at every direction in which they play.

I brandish my cockscomb and dance seductively round her
but she's so stuck with her brood she will not break free to me.

She will intuitively stay out and not come to roost if night falls
unless every chick she hatched comes in and clucks for recognition;

she will not sing except a mother's song, nor dance except with her chicks
nor cheerfully cry except when not one but all are giddily possessed.

She meticulously preens every chick's feathers male or female
before hers and most times has no time to beautify herself.

My muse is surely a mother hen with a large brood.

Heartbreaks

Without the unexpected silences that disrupt the ritual
without the long text messages that explain a hitch

without the motorcycle accident that burns the calf
without the dead phone batteries that refuse to charge

without the generators' switches that conspire to break
without the rain that deluges everywhere with worries

without the sun whose heat stokes sweat out of bodies
without Area Boys brandishing machetes and guns

without the running around that exhausts the entire day
without visits to the hospital, licensing office, and market

without waiting to no avail at the tailor's for party clothes
without the unannounced visitors that must be attended to

without the headaches that knock off the emotional radar
without assignments that close the mind to phone calls

without the preoccupation of carrying the sun in the heart
without falling asleep out of fatigue and missing the tryst

without complicating the already compounded complexities
without isolating the already distant island of solitary ones

the minstrel wouldn't be pausing here and there to exhale
the muse wouldn't be such a fairytale bride in the chamber.

Song of myself

1

The minstrel swears by his pen he loves her one hundred and ten percent.
She says she is not sure of that but satisfied with what she's given as her share.

The muse repeats to the minstrel he is a goat and at best a dog,
the minstrel does not call the muse animal names, goat or bitch.

He swears there's no sweetness anywhere else except her fleshpots;
she says *un-hun* and does not believe at all in the oath of the pen.

She believes he is capable of declaring every fleshpot the sweetest
and she's not sure the song of adoration pours from his heart or craft;

he's frustrated that the muse does not take his sacrifice for such
and she continues to say the goat will be goat the dog will be dog.

He does not call her names as she calls him from an array of animals;
he thinks a goat can be a goat without being goatish, a dog but not doggy.

To her the goat will continue to defecate even as he walks on the street,
the dog will always be distracted by the smell of bitches along his way.

He calls her *wahala** which she accepts he has caused her to be;
she asks him, "You think say I dey craze or I no get head?"

He only laughs and responds not to the crazy question;
he knows jealousy can drive one in a mindless course, no head.

They bicker night and day but in between episodes of fracas
they share the sweetest fruit that grows out of love on earth.

2

As the drunkard walks along, observers note his zigzag gait.
The world hears thunder reverberate with deafening echoes.

The man thinks of the cow he slaughtered for the woman
whom others would not give even a chicken for a feast.

He forgets the butterfly does not refuse flattery of its flowery feathers;
the bird preening her feathers to show off beauty needs praise-songs.

The beautiful one thinks her fidelity to an un-appreciating one is futile
when serenaded from all corners with songs that make her head swell;

she forgets the ram does not reject compliments of his gnarled horns.
The keeper of the gate needs recognition to stand firmer than ever.

They hear that man and woman are always bickering night and day
but they are such creatures that cannot live without each other;

no-one is there when they take the sting out of their tongues
and lose themselves in each other's intoxicating sweetness.

No-one sees milk enter the coconut and make it the envy of juices;
you may never see snake partners together but they still make love.

There's sweetness there if you search for it after the bitter streak;
there's so much abundance after to forget the long austere season.

He swears by the pen

He swears by the pen his only possession
—no mouth to move mountains as his mates.

He brags about writing lethal words to silence rivals
—when has the pen ever silenced the roar of lions?

What can be lethal in a pen to a multi-billionaire,
what is a pen in the assembly of strongmen?

Those who sing my many praise chants and line
my routes need no pen to compose my virtues;

you need billions and trillions and not a fountain pen
to win state contracts and ministerial appointments.

Let him write all he wants of poems, plays, and novels
but who cares to read what doesn't generate capital?

I am high chief of my kingdom in an oil-rich state,
he is pen master of a penniless caste of dreamers!

He invokes Soyinka his bearded god for everything
when we revere Dangote, Dantata, Odutola, and Ibru.

They can write for their kind scrounging for leftovers;
we worship real gods and hundreds of millions adore us.

He swears by the pen and brags about his songs sung
overseas and how strangers mob him as if a superstar

but a pen has no voice, no power where we launch
cash to accomplish our desires—even kidnap him!

How many elections have Soyinka and Achebe won
with their old pens not to talk of his Taiwanese pen;

how many in the National Assembly or lodges are mad
to swear by the pen that is the standard of failed ones?

He can grumble, petition, and do mischief with his pen
after we have spoken and taken action in our caucuses.

Let him come and see my wives the cream of the entire Africa
and take his pen to court or marry any woman worth her beauty.

Let him come to our parties and see my friends dressed
in their class with the finest cars and swear by his stupid pen!

Money surely amplifies my voice everywhere in the land;
it booms, it thunders—it is the roar of the lion in town.

The pen stifles his words into silence in the illiterate world;
the pen is no match at all for cash that speaks so eloquently.

He swears by the pen his only possession and he still brags
before us strongmen of the nation who make things happen.

If the poet were the butt of his own songs

If the popular poet were the butt of his own songs
how sharp would he hone his words to wound himself

if the pastor grew yams in a gas-flared farmland
how effective would his prayers be for fertility

if for a week I were my driver's servant
how incessant would be complaints of exploitation

if the dog put its master on a long leash
what human rights would not be violated

if the parrot locked its owner in a glittering cage
what keening would not fill the air to stifle the bird

if the herdsman were the goat or sheep
what distance would he not cover for foraging

if the poacher were the iroko or mahogany
who would not be condemned for willful murder

if the fisherman were the catfish or barracuda
what net would not violate the Geneva Convention

if the judge were the innocent sentenced to death
what grisly ghost would not be invoked to haunt him

and if the famous composer were the butt of his own songs
what consideration would give a sharper edge to laughter?

To the new wordsmiths

I wonder if our people still listen or just hear
what comes from mouths with forked tongues.

There are those declaiming whatever's in vogue—
I never knew so many baby imbongis fill the land;

they stump their hairless chests as new wordsmiths,
and they must be enjoying the cyber-world of tweets.

They care not for me sleeping over what comes out
of my mouth for days to achieve a minute's encore.

The market's now filled with under-ripened fruits
plucked there to upstage those waiting for fruits to fall,

but nothing's as divine as a ripe cherry fruit
that falls to its favorite; its luscious juice an elixir.

The child calls himself a man to gain applause
but asks a bearded one to crack the walnut for him.

Everyone is taking a singular path as snakes do
to prove one millennial; short-lived memory

and see children pass Ogun, Idoto, and Tamara
without pause in a journey without destination;

they laugh at me for prostrating before elders
whose paths brought me so far before clearing mine.

They meet themselves in Facebook and become friends,
worship themselves only to break up with insults on stage.

The new griots in ponds behave as if in an ocean, but despite
global glare are fish in a bowl of water that cannot wander far—

they glide on the surface and make amateur fishers happy
while those carrying wisdom in their heads refuge underwater.

Some even design costumes with dreadlock trademarks
while those they denounce wear regular like the rest.

There's a performance on stage, come and see for yourself.
I stand aside and watch the performers insult my caste.

Are folks in our midst listening or just hearing what
comes from mouths with forked tongues; harangues?

Gatherer of honey

Gatherer of honey, dispenser of pleasures
I enter town and the women are happy

all the birds on heat preen their feathers
to knockout colors and acquire mellifluous voices

they stampede to cosmeticians and hairdressers
they even know the tiniest braids cast a spell on me

they know one has to be singled out of the crowd
for crowning as the season's lucky pageant queen

they know that to ride on the knight's horse
one has to perform the spirit-possessing song

I love women as I love delirious fragranced flowers
I take my favorite to smack with infinite pleasure

they bare their breasts full of sorrow
they seek laughter to thrive in its stead

they want a chance to be taken for a muse
and be remembered in song forever

it is happiness for the sun to rise here today
it is the malady's course to be on the road next day

in the name of touring to perform songs
and suffering from an incurable malady

even the old and ugly still invoke their charms
for a chance to flirt to their hearts' content

they know the goat will not shun cassava leaves
they believe the parrot will not pass corn by

they care not if there's no master plan for the future
they believe that *now* can start what goes on forever

past midlife for a decade I am still not settled
with no family because of the wandering disease

I leave town and the men go for thanksgiving service
pastors invoke fire to consume the spoiler of women

their holiness cares not if I live a day longer
they say my kind infests town with contagion

still I manage to be welcomed warmly
wherever I arrive with my brand of smiles

men in town don't ask themselves why
their women leave them for a stranger

they should blame themselves for losing beauties
to a vagabond who laughs and plays with them

with him their exhilaration is divine
they come to him through any storms

I leave with gifts that would fill a ship
I know the men think they have been robbed

the women who line up to see or hear me
know not I am just words and voice

I cannot buy bread for them not to talk
of presenting my favorite a Honda Accord

they care not for my not giving them gifts
nobody quarrels that I forget Valentine's Day

they rob men multiple times to please me
they pray for me and not their partners

gatherer of honey, dispenser of pleasures
I enter town and the women are happy.

Your cleanliness astounds me

Your cleanliness astounds me; it goes all round,
cleansing every taint the body or soul suffers.

If you were led by a sensual spell into mud,
you came out and went for thorough cleansing.

"I am preparing to go for the morning service,"
and I see you confessing love for forgiveness.

Your cleanliness astounds me; it's all over you
cleansing every taint the sensual body suffers.

It's because you are so prone to dirt like every
other person that you determine to be so clean.

Fish that always lives in water can still smell; you
live in overwhelming dirt but determined to be clean.

Your neatness astounds me because it's all around,
cleansing every taint body or soul is bound to suffer.

You dismiss from your mind the multiple demons
that not only strip you naked but couple with you;

you turn your eyes away from the pageant of lewd
dancers you had cheered and practiced their steps

and go to service to immerse in holy water to wash off
taints the sensual body smacked you with for love's sake.

Your cleanliness astounds me; it's all over you
cleansing every taint the sensual body suffers.

After the child's carefree play in the yard,
the mother throws her into the bath to scrub clean,

after seeing what should not be seen but has to be seen
you turn to the bright light of God for respite from dark.

Your neatness astounds me; it goes all round,
cleansing every taint the body or soul suffers.

It's not the transubstantiated wafer or wine
that counts but immersing to rid the body of dirt

that as humans we are bound to attract and live soiled
and persisting to keep clean despite overwhelming dirt.

You clutch tenaciously to light evading overarching dark,
you love passionately and chase out soul-wrecking demons.

Your cleanliness astounds me; it's all over you,
cleansing every taint the sensual body suffers.

Family counselor

My mother appoints me her firstborn, and so
family priest, the counselor of my siblings

and I laugh impishly at tasking the sworn violator
to enforce codes; the vagabond to regulate behaviors.

Unknown to his credulous congregation, the priest
wrestles daily with the demons of his humanity

before a bemused Grandfather God watching all
and wondering what has become of his handiworks.

With a brother abandoning his wife for a concubine
he has kept close to heart for more than a decade,

what will I do to bring him back to be a family man;
what spell cast over him to recant the possessing love?

As firstborn, senior in the knowledge of fallibility,
I often stagger on as if that were my natural gait

but really suffering the parrot's angst of dancing
frontward and backward; unsure of where safety lies.

I still embark on it like many doomed missions;
the old woman knows not the ferocity of smokeless fire.

Family counselor, firstborn and priest, I will return
to the family gathering with a predictable report:

once the sapling shoots out, it withdraws not underground;
the pig's out of the fenced lot and is everybody's fair game

and I know firsthand the exhilaration of beleaguered love
and the resistance struggle that fuels it into incandescence.

My mother appoints me her firstborn, and so
family priest, the counselor of my siblings

and I wonder how the goat will condemn its kind,
or disrobe myself of priesthood and lose face!

Wayo man

Once you hail me a minstrel, poet of a kind,
I won't fault you for calling me *wayo** man.

Do I not fabricate tall tales, call them lies,
to be applauded by large theatre audiences

do I not turn facts to fiction, don't call them faction,
for readers to argue about them as one or the other

do I not swear by the pen that fiction is fact
factoring in gullibility of intelligent readers?

Have I not turned a drunkard into a teetotaler
to imbibe the calculating spirit of sobriety

have I not sent a woman into a men-only meeting
to chastise boastful patriarchs for their deficiency

have I not worn costumes and made ritual signs
to slip into secret societies to tap arcane knowledge

do I not pass for many people though I am one
with a name mangled out of joint by migration?

Once you hail me a poet, member of a proud caste
I won't fault you for calling me wayo man.

Am I not trainer of tortoises everybody wants to watch
in a country of one hundred and eighty million tortoises

do folks not know where I come from when I say
I am from the most prayerful but rotten country on earth?

How will I not be wayo man in a land whose women seek
only tall men and I wear hidden stilts to capture their fancy

and since men lose their heads to fair women my sister bleaches
with Ambi to catch a business tycoon who cannot cope with her?

How will the minstrel not be wayo man
if Tutuola sent a *drinkard* to bring his tapster from a dead town,

Okigbo ransacked Mesopotamian cemeteries and found Enkidu alive
and Soyinka took Ogun to Stockholm for the palm wine of their lives?

Once you hail me poet, member of a proud caste
I won't fault you for calling me wayo man.

How will I not be *wayo* man when I don't come last
in any competition whether I train for it or not Warri-style,

pass courses I did not register for and whose exams I did not write;
read unknown letters with candlelight in a dark OPEC country

how will I not be wayo man if my country is a giant
and I am only a rat without rights because I am not born to rule?

Just hail me minstrel, poet of a proud caste
and call me wayo man and not the worst of names.

---

* *wayo* man: Pidgin English for trickster, untrustworthy person, and whose character exhibits other negative connotations.

Acquittal

I won't give my muse a minute's sentence
however terrible the transgression

as she will not bring indictments against me
however vicious the violations;

what I do or she does cannot be criminal
even if it breaks laws of men and state.

However scandalous her *wahala*
I will not accuse her of breaking the peace

as whatever *wayo* game she catches me playing
she will not accuse me of any wrongdoing;

the court I constitute at the center of my heart
will select a jury to vindicate her innocence

and the court she sets up from the bottom of her heart
will sit a jury of my sympathizers and admirers.

Hostile witnesses may produce damning evidence
to the prosecution marshaling pay-back arguments

but the soft-spoken defense with heart aflame
will deploy poetry to turn the court to its side.

If I am accused of apostasy eloping with her
I will be declared freeing a captive from a kidnaper

and if the muse is accused of theft of a wandering man
surely she will be declared restorer of human rights.

Even if the rest of the world testifies against her
I will acquit her for having a true heart in her chest

and if the world holds me in contempt and wants me sentenced
only she will deploy the resources of love to set me free.

When her self-brewed tea cup burns my mouth
it indelibly brands inimitable love emblems on my lips

and if I spill hot water to scald her velvet thigh
I add to the panache of her secret beauty spots.

I won't give my love a minute's sentence
however terrible the transgression

as she will not indict me her true love
however vicious the violations.

Self-defense

They say I am the loafer, the stay-at-home one
and everybody smacks me with terrible insults!

When the warrior chief's home caught fire in his absence
I spotted it and alerted folks to stop the savage blaze;

when the wealthy farmer's mother took ill and collapsed
I, the reviled loafer, the stay-at-home one, revived her.

They call me the town's lazybones whose hands soft
like ripe bananas peel when I do the least hard work;

they call me the weak-kneed one so listless and feeble
I cannot jump across the creeks; what it takes to fish.

They say I haven't the bile it takes in the liver
to kill a snake not to talk of catching snakefish,

they say I am like rock salt used in preparing dishes
and would melt and so cannot fish or farm in the rain

but I am sent on errands, the town-crier of every season.
I composed the chant that makes leopards of warriors;

in days of Biafra I spotted camouflaged saboteurs
before military intelligence recovered from rape orgies.

I compose lethal songs that at every *udje* festival
destroy boastful rivals and make us invincible warriors;

of course our performers always take credit for them
as those like me everywhere dispossessed and silenced.

I am abused as a school dropout but I am the one called
to read letters of the educated to their abandoned parents;

they abuse me for not yet marrying but I take care
of wives the rich leave behind in pursuit of money.

They say I am the loafer, the stay-at-home one
and everybody smacks me with terrible insults!

I am so predictable

I have been too predictable
October tropical thunderstorm

comes late afternoon and spends its fury
before night falls

so predictable once the clouds thicken black
it is bound to fall or blow somewhere else to pour

I am so predictable
after many schools and travels

I break local taboos
without fear of any consequence

a man eating snails and not stammering
making love in daylight without albino children

I am so predictable
I am married with one wife

but exercising polygamous instincts
that the village DNA tagged me with

I am so predictable
ivory bangles

they are worn on the wrists
to show off wealth

so predictable are my lies
that I don't even tell them to my lover

who sees through me
like international airport scanners

I am so predictable
I was born a girl

it took five years for my father's
family to discover I am male

I am so predictable
my indecipherable thoughts remain unread

the epiphanies of daydreams
and the nightmares of joy

I am so predictable
nobody cares to come close to me

I am so predictable
nobody really knows me!

On the day of no prohibitions

They suspend the clan's merciless prohibitions for a day
to raise more than enough dust to cover the king's burial

(the earth will still know of his death however dusty the day
and the unadventurous will still not seize the indulgence);

they sanction brazen robberies and other violations,
they give the day to hooligans to exercise their craft.

Animal keepers, lock up your fowls, goats, sheep, and pigs;
today's violations however vicious bring no reprimand.

Merchants and traders, lock up your stores and sheds;
husbands of beautiful women, keep your jewels tight;

today there are no sanctions against eloping or kidnaping.
The knowing ancestors and gods allow humans anything;

they suspend the clan's merciless prohibitions for a day
to oblige predatory instincts to wear themselves out

and to cover the line of predators called kings in the clan
and announce the name of the next sinecure chieftain.

Of course I will saunter into town to seize what I covet
but have not—good to have royal privileges for a day!

Our forebears surely know how to care for the clan's poor,
they know vagabondage is not only mine but widespread;

they suspend the clan's merciless prohibitions for a day
for humans to forage the entire land to fill their desires

and to raise dust to cover the burial of a king whose life
has been to live on the clan, rob goats, pigs, and wives.

I like suspending our merciless prohibitions for a day
because that's the day I met my wife from the clan,

I took her away as my wife without asking questions;
we knew the chance of a lifetime on that special day!

Juju dance

If love were a juju dance, I would love without inhibitions;
wherever the dance led me meant my goddess possessed me.

If love came only as a thunderstorm of the peak rainy season
I would either drown or swim in overwhelming passion;

if love were farming, I would dig on till I became sore,
the harvest of the toil would not be measured in barns but banns;

if love were fruit-picking, I would enter the heart of the forest
and wander to wherever the hallucinating fruit ripened for me.

I would like my love to be a juju dance in an open field,
every step or gesture sanctioned by the possessing deity;

there would be no hurt gyrating on top of blazing charcoal.
I would tango with my partner through thorns or storms;

her beauty would possess me to serenade her in gibberish
that would make meaning to only the entangled two of us.

Surely my love is a tireless juju dance; it has no inhibitions
and the muse takes absolute credit for all my human missteps.

The emigrant

When at home I am the subject of all the abuse songs;
I leave town for a quiet living and it's the same abuse—

I am not the first senior child to emigrate nor will be the last;
our great grandparents founded Oshogbo* over a century ago.

It befuddles me, the outcry about my stay in town; it was not enough
my parents crossed the Ethiope here and I am a permanent immigrant;

it befuddles me because robbers and murderers are conferred
with chieftaincy titles; no song against theft from the commonwealth.

At home you deride me with all sorts of songs, chaser of women
who cannot resist the beauties that want the vagrant and lazybones.

Should I stay at home and take to drinking, have a harem that will
incapacitate me with daily bickering and a hundred children?

The python grown tired of the familiar forest of its birth slides
into the creek flowing into rivers that join the Niger for the ocean;

the cat, hunter of mice, tired of domesticity leaves the house for
the wilds another existence promising it the paws of a leopard.

Because I was a coward scared to death by the blood of
money-making rituals I fled the land of inescapable culture;

because I didn't want to rob or kidnap centenarians and babies
for ransom, I ran away not to be poor and disgrace my family;

because I did not want the National Assembly to be
the pinnacle of my career I flew out for another life.

Though out of home I know the new songs and dance steps
as you but you have no idea of the beauty I have seen outside;

one stuck in a hole cannot have a sharper mouth to laugh
than who knows what you miss as humans but don't know.

You will always have dirty songs to compose against me.
Now I pity you and make you the laughingstock of my song!

---

* Oshogbo, now in Osun State, designates migrant status in Urhobo since it was the favorite destination for many to pursue farming in ancient times.

Consolation

The god of short folks is tall so tall
up there his height touches the sky—

Napoleon is remembered for his size
and Pygmies forage forests of mahogany.

Softwood wears a cloak of thorns
to avert suffocating violation;

the Chihuahua's bark unsettles the warrior
to stop advancing on an undefended quarter.

Water and gin look so alike in a bottle that
you have to taste them to know the difference—

what douses fire and what sparks it
look the same; watery to the eyes.

Of course, generic copies wipe shame away
from my inability to pay the brand prices!

Did the healer not ask for only the feather
and not the entire parrot to cure my blockage?

I ran away from a cobra coiled on my doorstep
explaining it as the warrior fleeing to recoup—

he is not afraid when he hesitates or looks back
though sometimes even the brave fear a battle!

When rivals heard I shot a leopard in the forest,
they said a civet cat must have run into my trap

(it mattered not if the fortunate hunter caught
the terror of the jungle deep asleep and fired)

but when I wore the skin they shut their mouths;
my rivals shut their mouths but still clapped!

Ekanigbogbo*

After all these years Ekanigbogbo reappears
to still challenge me in a one-on-one game.

I tell the imaginary opponent I am no longer a child
but he says it doesn't matter the years I have grown

since last we competed in a series of games
and I won all despite trips that disadvantaged me.

"If you don't know, Teacher, an old man is a child,"
Ekanigbogbo lectures me in the class I designed

and equipped for lessons I thought I was sole expert of.
I am all ears to the partner I summoned to challenge me.

"If you beat me, then you pass judgment on yourself:
you are not good in what you teach others! You know

the warrior chief is sometimes afraid of battle. Will you
give up a fight against one you can trounce and be applauded?

Can you give up the anticipated applause and forego
the prize of rolling drums for the smiling champion?"

Ekanigbogbo is trying to distract me playing a fast
Muhammad Ali-on-Frazier on me—beat me

before the real contest will start and walk over me.
I do not give in to any threat or intimidation.

"You are wise—after all your name tells it all
but that's a carapace. The cricket knows it suffers

without thick armor. The porcupine still needs
a big heart even with its cloak of pine shafts!"

What have all these years taught me, years Ekanigbogbo
hibernated in a retreat at a workshop without a coach?

“You are as good as who you seek as your challenger,”
he tells me. Enough of saber-rattling! Let the game begin!

Not even the Olympics will stir this excitement of a challenge
between a sixty-something and his ageless opponent.

No false move escapes exploitation. Rule Number One.
He took advantage of my unguarded doorstep, a setback.

The rules ran on. Don’t underestimate your opponent
in any contest as you don’t underestimate your ability!

I am my own opponent in Ekanigbogbo’s strange court
and he fights with the resources of my stocked armory!

My rival carries my brain in a smarter fashion than me
because he never fails to take some steps ahead of me—

when I hold the patent of a lifelong task of research,
his generic works more effectively; his patent is often

my delayed thought. “I knew this,” I would exclaim
over what he surely stole wholesale from my head.

What game for two fierce antagonists without a referee?
We are not vying for the same office in a rigged election!

“If I am no longer a child, you are not invisible or imaginary,”
I taunt the taunting son of a bitch. If I could rattle his nerves,

at the worst a draw in a game either of us wants badly.
I forget the smart aleck I play with. “Have you heard of

Sudden Death, you knower of everything to be studied? Or
the Golden Goal, whatever it’s called? No draws anymore!”

I rethink of other strategies to counter who now plays
with the best of the skills that I don't even know I have!

"We are both prattlers in the game we boast of playing well.
Learn to lose so you can win! Win and lose. What do you want?"

"Of course I play to win. Don't continue to distract me," I say.
We engage in an epic battle over a trifle: lead the other to a pitfall!

"Will you give up what you hold dear if you lose this contest?"
"What do you have to wager on, stranger without a fixed address?"

Tit for tat is the name of the game for two lost in time and lost
in passion or desire and life where everything is 'yours' or 'mine'.

I reflected. If I beat my opponent I will lose my wager.
Then I should lose to win. Lose if playing alone to win!

---

* *Ekanigbogbo*: in Urhobo folklore is one's imaginary opponent that always loses every game.

The new lotus eaters

(after a three-week stay in Abuja)

They leave home lean of body after selling all they have
of material and spirit to win the people's mandate to rob;

they arrive in Abuja or any of the satellite capital cities
refuged in lavish rooms a world away from tribal shacks.

Once there they transform without effort into goats, pigs,
pythons, and other beasts scrambling in the oil-glutted soil

for what only non-humans care for as the meaning of life;
they are practically animals without human minds and souls.

They forget what they were sent there for, to fight battles
that will give dignity to their people as human beings;

the representatives forget they are messengers of hope
to bring succor to desperate folks languishing in despair.

They hide in their paunches the billions meant for roads
and bridges that will take desperate people out of misery.

Obese in the cult of theft they are sworn to by Speakers,
they waddle in pleasure and wander no more to seek cures

for folks at home being strangled by multiple afflictions;
they no longer remember the message they came with

because they live in the land of lotus eaters, capital city;
brains anomied from the deliciously intoxicating wine

they share constantly as their dividend of democracy;
night and day they distill wine from lotus to consume.

They invite marabouts and other fetish priests to their dens
to save them from being lynched by demons of their lust;

they know not that the thief will never enjoy peace or safety—
he will forever be hounded by enraged spirits of stolen wealth!

Soon incapacitated, most die where they had been sent to fight;
they are already dead and buried in infamy in their new homes;

others possessed by the diabolic aroma of the lotus
and the loot they frolic in die like their kind, vultures.

Surely, there's no island here to grow abundance of lotus
but thanks to oil, the land's awash with the hallucinating plant

and in his wandering the minstrel watches the population
and swears not to make the city of lotus-eaters his home.

They say my child is ugly like a goat

They mock me because of my child
whom they say is ugly like a goat.

Don't mind them who see nothing good.
My pickin* fine pass any goat.

Where are the mockers when my child
fetches water and runs errands for me?

They mock me because of my child
whom they deride as ugly like a goat.

Don't mind who see only ugliness.
My pickin fine pass any goat.

They have no child of their own.
They do not even rear a goat.

Don't mind my avid mockers.
My pickin is a sweet darling.

---

* pickin: Nigerian Pidgin English for child.

Learning

"We have seen many of such," the old say,
to caution youths so exuberant in their passion;

every experience lurks in some proverb
and there wisdom to learn in a lifetime.

So, a non-traditional student I am learning.
I am still naïve in the purview of experience;

I still fall into the pit in daylight and no light
shines bright enough to free me from missteps.

I had thought being kind was enough good
but bad turns easily brought regrets to it all;

to those I was generous mine were acts of folly.
I have not been able to resolve how not to be

a fool when everybody including me seeks wisdom.
How will I remain human without foolish deeds?

Let me be cautious so as not to be a fool again
and I postponed like one who controls the future

until one a pittance would have saved died;
one I could save with company died of solitude

and lives a full bucket from my well would
have hydrated succumbed to prevailing drought.

I wanted the fruits in my garden to ripen
so well until the juice became an elixir

but worms stole in as if watching my delay
for a foretaste that poisoned my appetite.

My neighbors were quick to compose a song
to laugh at laziness and procrastination.

I had no answer to their beautiful but evil song—
it was my own calculations that betrayed me.

I went on to plant Lokoja yam king of kings
and waited to harvest prize-winning tubers

but beetles dug into them as if theirs
and so corrupted and ruined my chances.

Neighbors laughed at me with a new song
they made sure I heard over and over again:

The miserly one eats only beetle-ravaged yams!
Not harvesting his yams, beetles helped him out!

How do I counter a song so proverbial I was struck
dumb? I could not sing back with the same talent.

I confess to knowing no single way to please all,
since no one dish will be praised by all the tasters

who come to my party with different notions
of grandeur and none wants mine better than his.

Yes, not knowing made me a tortoise
rather than the human being I am.

O muse, inspire me to be impulsive in giving
out of the gifts I receive—all I own are gifts;

let me not calculate any profit or loss of deeds
but let my investments be sacrifices for good.

"We have seen many of such," the old say.
I know learning is a lifelong school. I am still at it.

III

Songs of the Homeland Warrior

In memory of Isaac Adaka Boro and Ken Saro-Wiwa

Survival is a just war.
The war is here; the war is now!

(Ademola Dasylva)

If those called militants

If those called militants
had *The New York Times* or *The Times of London*
they would call their detractors unprintable names

if the laboring poor
had the power to overturn their suffering
they would make servants of their lords

if animals in the bush
had firepower of their own
they would teach hunters a mortal lesson

if free-ranging chickens
had steel claws in their armory
they would impale every hawk that swoops down

if the homeland warriors called militants
had their own CNN and Aljazeera
they would call their robbers monsters

they would ask nations
why they fought for independence
from occupiers of their lands

they would ask peoples
why they fought against enslavement
to enjoy their freedom

they would ask them all
enough questions to embarrass them
and prick their benumbed conscience

into waking from villainy
into the realization that what's
good for them is also good for others!

If they had their gods here

If they had their gods here
if they buried their ancestors here
if their totem pet roamed here
if their muse drank from here
if their arts were inspired by this landscape
if they raised their children in this community
if they made their living from this soil and water
if they exercised their leisure here
if this land affirmed their humanity

they would use the most offensive weapons
in their secret arsenal
they would employ the meanest tactics
that defy the Geneva Convention
and care less for whatever obscenities
the rest of the world hurled at them
they would battle even harder to victory
if the abused bounty was theirs
and their violators insulted them as militants.

Can i still call from the River Nun?

Can I still call from the River Nun to the sea maids
lounging in the Atlantic to come to me for a party

can the river bird still be heard and summoned
to perch and dance on the reed in the tide

can the legendary labyrinths of the Delta
take the fisherman to work and back with songs

can the endangered iroko, mahogany, and others
hold back the fire of the conglomerate of poachers

can the warthog, porcupine, deer, and dozens of game
defend themselves against the army of developers

can the fish population fondly called children of the gods
stop the poisoning of their resident water by oil workers

can the green leaves, grass, and teeming undergrowth
shield themselves against the toxic flames of arsonists

can the air that sustains the living in this blessed portion
insulate itself against the vagabond flares of raging gas

can the soil under assault from fires set by money mongers
find relief from its tormentors in corporate headquarters

can the rains, God's lavish draughts for needy folks,
escape the black clouds of fumes blanketing the sky

can night, refuge after the day's toil, now in flames
regain its dark shade and maintain its cool dominion

can residents of the divine gardens of plenitude
survive perils of dollar lords at Abuja and abroad

can the remnant population of the abused land still
live meaningful lives after the death of companions?

Let those insulting defenders of their haunted homeland
answer the questions posed by whom they call militant!

Don't follow the palm wine tapper's course

Don't follow the palm wine tapper's course
that's on everybody's lip in song:

Odjoboro is strong but foolish—
he built his canoe with soft wood

when there's abundance of hardwood in the forest
for a sturdy canoe to ply creeks and rivers.

Our folksongs lie to the young of today
who see nothing even of soft wood

not to talk of hardwood or forest
and no rivers left in the land to ply!

In the Omoja River

In the Omoja River we washed body and tools,
as we crossed from the farm after the day's task.

There too, young, we listened to murmuring water
before taking tracks into the forest to pick fruits;

the sun wriggled between leaves whose shadows
danced on water; a spectacle of correspondence.

But they brought affliction to the cheerful river;
they brought flames of fear to the marvelous forest:

they pissed and pissed barrels of arsenic into the current
until it is no longer the ageless river sung but a cesspool;

they stripped and stripped the forest naked of its ever-
green suit until it is no more a forest but a sand-field.

When young grandparents return to the spots where
we deflowered, nothing remains to excuse the love.

Gone, the cool mat of leaves on which we stretched
and the green canopy that even in rain did not distract.

You can imagine what we wish despoilers of the land—
what we wish the world's criminals and transgressors!

Much of the year wet

Much of the year wet, it lives a regular life
in royalty in the creeks, streams, and lakes;

the mudfish floats with a retinue of family
fins, and from its gestures must be partying.

Baits dropped by fishers fill the water but
it averts hook and net, going for plankton.

In the dry season often a castaway
in dusty creeks ensconced in mud,

a living miracle of drought, it settles
down to live a recluse's life to survive.

Fish holed in low water-level earth,
the rains will always come to free it

from the dungeon of dust, not a grave
but only a diversion to the fishermen.

In early hurricanes in the village we caught
mudfish that we thought fell from the sky,

and Grandma concurred to please us
to make us grow and learn with age—

with the Atlantic at the horizon and dry
creeks staring, we looked over the fact!

It turned out to be the tastiest fish;
no wonder it was compared to sex:

the man making love with a woman
seen as mudfish sliding into a cone-net!

Singular fish a monarch metamorphosed
into, he possessed unfathomable power

he exercised over nobles and commoners.
The king of fish, none contests its primacy.

Should I choose to be fish in the next world,
would I survive in the methane-filled streams?

Only in his memory

Only in memory
thrive the affluent residents of the wetlands:
the black anthill that wears a conical helmet
the *oko* bird escorting the current after first rains to the sea
the flutter of butterflies that fills the farm with pageantry
the armada of newly hatched fish in sailing formations
the sleek creeks in flowing sheets cutting across the forest
the double-lined mangroves providing honor guard to boaters.

Only in his memory
the exuberance of his irrecoverable youth
where he still hugs green-garmented herbs
kisses the beauties that converge on the rain-flushed land
waves tall grasses dancing to the wind's polyrhythm
swoons before the full moon and attendant stars
immerses in the divine bath of thundering storms
and walks the soil murmuring soothing chants to his soles.

Now he carries scars of burns
watches his companions afflicted with toxic fumes
hears no more the multiethnic orchestra of the wilds
witnesses the vast grove stripped of its divine garment
and the rest no mirror of his youth.
And only in memory brought alive in dreams
does he recover and walk a stranger to himself
that the homeland warrior recognizes his lost land.

At Eruemukohwarien

At Eruemukohwarien*
designated *Ughelli 1*
bold on oilfield charts
but never on road maps
stealing past police guards
beside flow stations
with a phone camera
wriggling through bush
onto a metal platform
I took close shots
of two gas flares
that have been burning
for fifty years and for sure
will go on for centuries
if the earth's not exhausted.
Beside the twin infernos
a wilted cassava farm
that cannot feed a child
and blackened earth denying
plants and creatures life
with the heat hell promises
those committing mortal sins
in a silenced community
begging for sentry work
from its tenants
now lords of the land.

---

* Eruemukohwarien: a small town close to Ughelli in Nigeria's Delta State with several oil wells.

The zestful river lost its fine fingers

The zestful river lost its fine fingers
that once pointed to ancestral wetlands

to a sluice of oil-borne toxins seeping
through the skin to dissolve membranes.

The forest that for long stood erect has its
legs amputated by multinational poachers

to post proud profits at the Stock Exchange;
the refuge of green vandalized by intruders.

All the groves and beauty spots disfigured
by constant exposure to acid showers.

You wouldn't know this was the primeval haven,
this home whose residents drop from agonies—

fishermen and other folks fell to Bell's seduction
and now survive only on imported frozen fish!

The smooth body lacerated beyond recognition
by gas flares and blowouts; the skin peels away.

The anthills marking the land sank into oblivion
from perennial corrosion; the body damned crust.

The catfish wears no whiskers, as the mudfish misses
its phallic head; both now alien in their home waters.

The homebred parrot no longer spokesman of birds,
just as the burning sky rid the eagle of its majesty.

The eyes of the earth, blinded by convulsive fumes,
no longer the sentinels that kept us safe at a distance;

only one ear not two opening to all directions
and so no more forewarns of advancing perils;

the nose a mere facial protrusion and the tongue
a labial outgrowth; no longer the household taster.

These mutations stuck with us, so inescapable;
accursed fate of bartering one wealth for another.

The multitude of fish

The multitude of fish used to express gratitude
to the creeks and streams for their hospitality.
Today the oil-soaked residence holds no such life.

The birds now live in fear of no nests to return to;
in flight they head away from smoldering winds.
The winged ones have lost their unassailable height.

The undergrowth swarmed with a world of its own,
but now regular blowouts and flares burn the forest.
The scarred population is sad it lost its green refuge.

The day now wears soot over its broad face
and returns not with its cheerful presence.
The sun laments the loss of its bright dominion.

The moon can no longer brag about its bounty.
At night gas flares rob it of magnificence;
at no time can it exercise its rights in the dark.

The air sweats from uncontrolled fires and toxins;
the breeze no longer a fan but a blowing firebrand.
The air is reeling from the smoke-smothering rack.

The soil that soothed homeboy soles to be so agile
no longer the cool comforting company sought.
The soil sick from blowouts, we groan from burns.

The sky that once dispensed abundant light and rain
now lives infuriated with fumes in a troubled state.
The sky looms overhead without its generous smile.

One yam from the farm used to feed a family for a week
and herbs cured serious ailments without hospital charges.
The people are dying from the loss of divine sustenance.

There was a time you followed the water queen to her palace,
walked on the current since no boat and you couldn't swim.
The new country of prayers invokes in vain spiritual power.

You made it to God so high to petition for your needs
and the abused orphan brought his mother back to life.
The oil lords drown supplicants in loud reports of gunfire.

The glorious land of plenitude in folksongs
used to praise the good luck it was blessed with.
Today, it weeps lavishly in the afflicting dearth.

I pass the same roads

I pass the same roads the Bekederemos* have passed,
stand at the crossroads of sacrifice to invoke Tamara*
to avenge the wrongs done to them and the land.

I listen to the lyrics of dark arbor-lined creeks of fish
and the orchestra of every bird and life of the mangroves
but hear only hisses of fuming flares at multiple locations.
I look up to the sky to address the invisible powers
and seek the blessings of ancestors that gave Ozidi*
the fortitude of heroes and Kenule* brave martyrdom.

With all my breath I call the water queen whose love is
my fortune the sea continues to replenish for a lifetime.
I call her attendant mermaids that serenade her majesty
but the oil supertankers berthed deep in the horizon
afflict the beauty with sickening slicks and sluices.

Tell me the day of the year that the sun will smile
and not confused with worries of smothering fumes,
tell me when the moon in its anticipated outing
will not hide deeper than the stars amidst the soot
mountains of refineries covering the neighborhood;
tell me the season of organic cherries or other fruits
with the soil soaked full of methane and toxins.

Whether I hurry or tarry at the outskirts of town,
it matters not when I arrive with no fresh fish
to treat my favorites or the food market to sell.
The town is stripped of regattas and masquerades.

I pass the same roads the Bekederemos have passed,
stand at the crossroads of sacrifice to invoke Tamara
to avenge the wrongs done to them and the land.

To those spreading afflictions, Tamara, strike them
with loathing for the harm they do without qualms.

---

* Bekederemo: prominent Ijo family of the Clarks in Kiagbodo, Delta State of Nigeria.
* Tamara: Ijo for God.
* Ozidi: Ijo epic hero.
* Kenule: Ken Saro-Wiwa, environmental and minority rights activist executed by the Sani Abacha regime on November 10, 1995.

Come and spend a day with me

Come and spend a day with me

see my wife close to her term
see me preparing for my first-born
see my mother waiting for her grandchild
we pray night and day for a safe delivery
after many miscarriages and complications
always on our knees for a healthy baby
after so many malformed births around
continuously invoke the ancestors
after encountering strange happenings
in the land that raised us to this day

come and experience the life we live
and see for yourself the rigors we bear
and tell others the tale of our blues.

I had left home with reluctance

I had left home with reluctance and while away
yearned daily for the beauties and abundance
I had abandoned; blamed myself for ever leaving.
And to regain my peace, I gathered all I had acquired
and back I set out for the sweet home of plenty where
I expected to wear the garlands of happiness for life;
the fugitive swallowed pride, a rehabilitated prodigal.

But what a startling revelation awaited me at home!
Ghosts of all kinds welcomed me to the homeland:
evergreen ghosts standing beside wilted branches
leaving an arboreal graveyard of an entire forest;
ghosts of the game tribe crowding forlorn ruts
now slick routes snaking their way into nowhere;
ghosts teem vacuous holes of abandoned anthills,
ghosts of iguanas and falcons now on sentry duty.

And these are not the ghosts of murderers that will
raise alleluias on the lips of every saved person
but of the innocent mowed down in the crossfire;
artillery exchange between oil lords and resource
warriors; surely they are not the resurrected saints
whose fresh features will be embraced as new culture
but ghosts of everlasting dirges bewildering the living
and the dead with none with a refuge to call theirs.

Wherever I turn at my homecoming, ghosts
that deny the basic necessities of life and
lead away from playgrounds to scorched earth
intensifying desperation with dearth and sickness.
At homecoming in place of embracing homefolks
I turn back to raise an army to rout ghosts and
reinstate life where death has poached a number.

On whose side is the truth?

On whose side is the truth in this matter;
in whose heart does the land bleed and hurt?

On whose side does truth tenaciously cling
in the tugging war that ravages the land?

In whose head does the land chronically ache?
Who suffers the multitude of afflictions?

Who sings the dirge of rivers and forests
infested with ghosts of children of gods?

Who laughs at the wake of my neighbors
whose demise raises stocks to the heavens?

On whose side is truth ranging in the land,
with mourners or celebrants of deaths?

Those blinded by lust devastate beauty
without knowing the extent of the hurt.

Victims of such a massive assault as this
never hold back on mauling the intruders.

Those who hurt and humiliate others,
what truth can they find in their hearts?

Those who control armies and capital
and believe they are forever invincible,

how do they know in their benumbed hearts
that they fool themselves with falsehood?

How far can they see to comprehend that
invisible powers look on from above them?

Maybe they are right

Maybe they are right who say my rage is misdirected,
that I should fight first those from the same home;

they say that I fold my arms and look on without seeing
my lavish portion taken by chiefs and representatives

in the name of the community I cry is so marginalized
and by those who take away the huge share on its behalf.

Those who insult me point fingers back at my people
who cry with me at home but smile with them at Abuja;

my rightful share's hoarded in local and foreign accounts
by those who appear to cry with me but not on my side.

They say it's not that I don't have more than enough to alter
my plight but I allow those who claim the share to squander it

in palaces, cars, and consorts that mock the community's want;
they do not bring home a fraction of the share meant for us.

My representatives at the big table where the sharing takes place
don't bring home whole the largesse we more than deserve;

those who step forward as chiefs and go to the capital cities
have only their bags to fill and nothing for the communal coffers.

Maybe I sit down and look on while chiefs and representatives
hurl away from the House our portion to have their appetites sated

and starting the war from the home ground before moving out
will save the bountiful land from starvation and annihilation.

Maybe they are partly right on the share from the big table.
But how can they be right on the wasteland on which we live?

If I were to ask my people

If I were to ask my people
what they wanted the most,
they would definitely choose
money over every other thing,
including good health and peace
that I know there's a dearth of
because of oil and gas everywhere
that by right should bring us wealth.
If I were to ask them what they
would do to be free of the hell
that stops them from being farmers
or fishers that fend for themselves,
they would pray, sow seeds for
prosperity, and surrender what's
left to pastors for more prayers;
hence you can call me militant
for standing in front for them
who would grumble loud but dare
not raise their fists against thieves.

We dey chop akara dey go

We dey chop akara dey go
if moin-moin no dey

we ask for resource control,
Gov'ment give us NDDC*

We dey chop akara dey go
if moin-moin no dey

in place of clean rivers,
Shell dey build boreholes

We dey chop akara dey go
if moin-moin no dey

we seek development for the community;
they build service roads to flow stations

We dey chop akara dey go
if moin-moin no dey

they hanged our standard-bearer
and made 2 I/C of a nincompoop

We dey chop akara dey go
if moin-moin no dey.

---

* NDDC: Niger Delta Development Commission.

So many questions

So many questions I can't answer.

After all the birds fall silent in the delta,
how can there be Rex Lawson*
with the polyrhythm of weaverbird, sunbird,
carpenter-bird, solos and ensembles?

After the woodpecker slips underground,
the hyrax fallen still from flares
and all the voices of the land muffled,
how can there be Rex Lawson again?

After the *oko* bird no longer fills the creeks
with *okotudun okotudun*,* the water drums
and currents clogged by spills and blowouts,
how can Rex Lawson's voice rebound?

After the earthworm has been poisoned
with seepage and percolation of wastes,
after the insect population has been decimated,
who can be a maestro without natural mentors?

Without snakes, iguanas, agamas,
how can a bard carry the polyrhythm
that made highlife a national treasure
to sing and dance to with our bodies?

Without the wind and currents,
the murmuring and lapping water, and
the spluttering fish, how can Rex Lawson's
voice be regained in Shell-shocked silence?

Who can sing without models of the forests?
Who can lisp God's wild children's voices

amidst flares, wheezes, and hisses? How can
Rex Lawson resurrect with a sweeter voice?

So many questions I surely can't answer.

* Rex Lawson—late great highlife musician of the Niger Delta.
* *okotudun okotudun*: onomatopoeic sound made by the *oko* bird following currents as the heavy rains start in the Niger Delta.

In the theater of war

In the theater of war, death ambles after life
for heroism in the mangrove swamps. See
the torched camps, villages, and waterways—
water fuels fire before falling as a downpour,
and then who can tell blood from oil sludge?
The theater changes, now a sprawling kingdom
and soon an expanse of rubble; not Gbaramatu*.
No cocks crow; the dead cannot wake to flee
coordinated assaults into refugee trails of tents.
In Warri the dance of death raises songs of sorrow
at the waterfront; the port peopled with ghosts.
The theater shifts from silent national newsrooms
to foreign media with the brush of Guernica
painting the massacre that shocks country folks—
bombarding fishing camps to kill militants;
obliterating squatters dialoguing with monkeys.
Calls come from far and near, asking "Are you
safe?" There's no safety anywhere in the land;
creeks, savannah, and lands of gorges and heights.
The cleansing intensifies with Abuja legislators
crying: "Flush them out also in Bayelsa and Rivers!"
To them, they are militants who cry foul of Bell Oil.
At the international court, let them plead guilty
to the crime of fueling fire; nailed by complicity.
The theater of war is a pool of blood; the rubble,
fueled by oil and gas, a wasteland; not Gbaramatu.

---

* Gbaramatu: an Ijo town in the creeks of Nigeria's Delta State that was repeatedly bombarded by the Nigerian military seeking to eliminate so-called militants.

In wake keeping

In wake keeping
we cast jokes to cheer the heavy heart

in the midst of hostility
we make love to reinvigorate ourselves

in the dirge-filled atmosphere
we sing blues and drink songs

we who are marginalized
flaunt ourselves at center stage

in the wide expanse of pain
we seek acreage of relief

despite the aches
we saunter on with vigor

in the gloom
we dream of resplendence

our potent weapon is not in Camp 5*
not assault rifles, grenades, or bombs

it's the humanity we refuse to cede
to those who would make us inhuman

by making us respond
to their challenge without our virtues

without what makes our life
the source of envy.

We respond to escalating war
with intensifying love.

* Camp 5: Tompolo's camp destroyed by federal troops in a combined air and sea assault.

For the wind that still blows

For the wind that still blows
and the *eyareya* grass that dances

for the day that still dawns
and light that covers horizon to horizon

for the night that still falls
and the respite in its refuge

for the voices of day and night that still ring
and the music to the ears

for the rain that still pours
and the green it engenders

for the seasons that still follow one another
and the regularity they provide

for the water that still flows
and the promise of entering the sea

for the sun that still rises
and the brilliance that sets in

for the soil we still walk and work
and the firmness of our gait

for the acres on which we still build
and the increase we accommodate

for the flowers that still flourish
and the crops to be harvested

for the bounty that still remains
and the famine kept at bay

we smile
and laugh

we sing
and dance

we play
hide and seek

we love
and make love

we dream
and hope. . .

IV

Secret Love and Other Poems

we learn from exhilaration that love leaves us lonesome

The painting suite

(To the muse of beautiful pictures)

1. *Beautiful Figure, Beautiful Landscape*

A beautiful landscape is an oil painting
of divine hands dipped into a rainbow trough

and splashed in possessed frenzy over the land;
a frame paints the history of antediluvian nature,

a miracle trough that's a bath for seeking birds
preening plumes and oiling throats for a gala;

a pageant that goes into the record of the sheer
beauty of the body of songs, a swooning trance.

A landscape of twin hills and a gorge painted
beautifully is a print work retched from wandering;

a beautiful figure conjured to a landscape
makes a beautiful painting for all times—

beauty of nature begets beauty of art in perpetuity;
a colorful canvas every judge nods at in deference.

My gift painting is a congress on a canvas,
a reunion of birds at a magic stream of colors;

a tapestry of thoughts and actions in yearnings
summoned to freeze in perpetual celebration.

We can kill an antelope and skin it
for a drum to echo into distances;

the hunter brings down the elephant
and the tusk speaks for generations—

the painting will not rust, ivory and diamond
in cooperative smoothness and roughness

fence off termites whose armies gather for assault
leaving the image secure in its contours for all times.

2. *Framed Painting*

This oil painting startles me to swoon; rite
of passage, delivery of deep yearnings:

life-sustaining spring out of bare-bodied rock;
a stream for birds to preen their plumes.

The painter is a magician delivering colors
and I seek currents to whet my songs.

You splash the gray day with radiance;
a flash of vision in permanent pose.

You stretch out your hands of olives
to uncover a warm dish for divinities;

oil loosening limbs to litheness, you
are masseuse of the spirit of grand décor.

I throw an egg to light the gorge to find and
haul away a cache of dark-swathed diamond

and today I absorb the softness of the egg;
smooth albumen we seek for its cleanliness.

With the oil painting framed to deck
the shrine for daily worship, I look up

to the sun's infinite fanfare of celestial fire;
lamppost and mirror reflections of a figure.

I will not call this painting by any name
since none I sing out will escape mobbing;

I will muster the minstrel's craft of magic
to smother the painting with praise-chants:

what fuels the sun to meet yearnings;
spring water cooling rock climbers!

3. *Chamber Painting*

The door opens the house to a cache of memories;
the chamber a bedrock of what money cannot buy.

The painting flares; despite the humidity around
it bristles with the resonance of a kept promise.

A framed painting seeks hanging by caring hands,
a pendant so rich in diamond and lined with ivory;

the muse is mindful of what to give out of fantasy
so that the eager minstrel is not reckless in his flight.

Two hands put together a pageant in a frame,
the painting now hangs in their open house.

The painting minimized into a pendant in their watch,
let them awestruck hold it steadily; exhilarating beauty.

4. *Drums for the Painting*

Without the lavish generosity of the muse
no majestic drums for the minstrel

without the faith and daily worship
there's no divinity in the deity

without the possessing percussion of the maestro
no reechoing applause for the master dancer

without the costumed figure
no portrait for the hallway of fame

without the haunting landscape
no painting for the galleries

without the long partnership
no reunion to celebrate

without one there
no other here

and for the exceptional glamor
I roll out these big drums.

Secret love

I

I am transferring my secrets into an unreadable script
but with careful study will reveal right from wrong.

I have hauled a gift painting to the chamber of treasures,
muddled my way in miasmic mud to the brightest of gems.

Demons torment my body with flameless fires
that no sophisticated radar detects in clear weather.

Don't let science fiction take over our lives from us;
those coming will live the fantasies of today's brains.

The slogan is a script that gives the politician a new image
and before you know it he assumes the meaning of the name

hence beware of the names you give or call loved ones—
call others lizards, wood, anything from the dictionary;

distance yourself from the eschatological sacrilege of names;
keep multiple poles between you and the wishes of witches!

II

Love becomes so lonesome it looks for someone to lean on,
in hunger it becomes voluptuous with damnable manners;

it seeks diversions everywhere with life-or-death desperation
that politicians are so adept at they exhort compatriots to arise;

it rehearses expressiveness at *The Ajakpa School of Rhetoric*
and now performs without effort *I love you!* to loud ovations.

The voice of endearment is a bounty of dissimulated echoes;
its knowledge a cherry tree incapable of fruiting in season.

I am saluted as commander of an armada of a dry-sea fleet
after promotion and decoration as captain of a phantom boat.

My temple is an abandoned dark cave whose spiders thread
for me a grey mantle to cover gross nudity from the public.

III

Don't break the table's legs and expect to sit eating on it,
or break both bottle and glass and still toast with the wine!

A tale meanders like forest paths but it goes to a destination;
the meaning of life is what we live in dancing to its rhythm.

Favor is a plant providing shade in the fire-breathing sun;
rotting, the tree falls and will fail to shield from the blaze.

The vast carcass of the elephant costs less than its ivory;
one song blessed by the muse compels the world's ears.

I am favorite of the gods the fortunate one sacrifices
to get to the bosom of the divine heart he worships—

others swagger to the platform to sing with a flourish,
I keep night awake with revisions for a minute's encore.

I will not bring home honey with a swarm of live bees—
amalgamation came with independence and civil war!

Bless the river that breaks through the forest,
bless the road that cuts across the market!

IV

I pitch my battle tent at the great crossroads of the land.
I cannot be wrong and right; either acquitted or convicted.

I stand between the two contestants for sovereignty,
bemused by their separate passions in the matter.

Whatever I do is taking sides with a guide who counsels
me to live through the torment and not run into a riot

crossing internal borders without stirring external bothers;
it will matter not where I live to deal with the two factions.

What virtues are not vices in the friendship I strike;
what vices are not virtues in the muddled life of love?

Now I have to devise a meeting in a neutral ground
to reconcile opposing factions that want me on their sides.

The court holds in the beleaguered cathedral I build
and I provide prosecutors and defenders from the same

pool of supporters and antagonists, a jury of sentimental peers—
I live at the judge's mercy; one judge two different robes.

V

The iroko reincarnates not into a lion, nor deer into pine;
the kind follows the same trail, call it dynasty or DNA

yet I praise the swordfish that impales the crocodile,
I praise women breaking into men's-only lounges;

praise the poor for seizing privileges of their lords—
none condemned to subjection in the new scripture.

I won't sit or stand still in the vortex defining today's life;
the gods bless with abundance of what our prayers seek.

The sun will rise from the east however long the night;
one season however weird must give way to another—

in youth I knew every year would steal something from me;
in age I earn more for songs so deep they threaten drowning me.

I prayed for paper and pen as all I needed for minstrelsy
but now the magic notepad has turned things upside down.

I weave more gently but beauty astounds more than ever.
Homage to path-breakers to springs to survive droughts

and where in the forest abundant fruits repulse famine's ogre;
they deserve the memorials we build with fanfare of songs.

I paint memorials of beautiful days to exorcize nightmares,
printing almanacs of pageants to always keep beauty alive.

I am transferring today's wishes into secret scripts
that with learning will bring delight to the absurd.

In contest

Relating with my muse is so complex
that she is scared of me as I am of her.

Once she possesses me, I do things
beyond my comprehension and power;

things I care not a minute's qualm
are right or wrong but I have to do.

I am scared of her as she must be of me;
she inspires what she complains about.

Each swears acting in the spirit of love
that runs them off the conventional track.

She deliberately nudges me to wander far
to catch me outside the nest and rail at me.

Once there's peace of millennial proportion,
some strife flares up and I know it is she

who wants no war but bored to death by quietude.
She berates me for throwing stones in our pond.

I am afraid of her secret resources a boon to me
as she is afraid of mine she considers a blessing.

Two mortals taunt one another to divine treats,
and the perpetual dread of life without the other.

For sure I relish stepping over the line she draws
as she does the line I show her to avoid crossing

but sovereignty has become each one's challenge
to be free and yet bound in the other's embrace.

"You are too smart for your own good!" she says,
and I know not whether compliment or scolding.

"You are too credulous of what you hear," I tell her
and she knows not whether out of candor or cunning.

Our relationship has grown to be so complex
she is scared of me as I am also scared of her.

For the muse of peace

Celebrating peace with a cool head is less flamboyant
than memorializing battles of bombs and bloodshed

with fanfare that with pomp and pageantry extols
the wrongheaded deeds we ought to sanction fast.

Today the minstrel outs his resources to serenade
the impossible distance covered without breakdown.

For now there are no conflicts or battles left to fight
but reposing in the serenity of the peace we cherish,

there are no more cries of blatant intrusions into
one's sovereignty in the prevailing Pax Africana;

no noise except the spontaneous outburst of laughter
breaking soothing silence to tease or tickle each other;

no headaches, backaches, or other self-inflicted maladies
but spritely agility of a bubbling body craving for touch.

All the resources expended to garner weapons of MD
now deployed to hold hands and entertain the other,

all poisons assembled to destroy the other detoxified
now creative agents spill out to lift the other's spirit;

all the energy wasted in souring the other's appetite
now harnessed into a charm that blows the heart away.

Without wrangling the muscles of the body relax
the body groomed to vibrate, a self-playing lute.

There's excitement of a new era sweeping through
the republic of love that has seen its share of troubles,

the river is calm as it has never been before now
since a stormy weather accompanied us from start;

the roads are smooth and wide throughways
and nobody complains of obstacles on the way.

The buoyant faces of fellow travelers tell the gains
of the new dispensation, the gains of experience:

now the lioness seduces with her trademark mane
and the partner sucks her milk, an invaluable elixir

and the ram fondles lavishly with his horns
and carries his partner in his silken forearms.

Let them prance gallantly in each other's arms
to the garden they have planted for themselves!

No more burns from arsonist skirmishes or ambushes,
no wounds; only free movement in the beautiful land

they compete to deck with flowers colorful and alluring
they weave adorable garlands to adorn the other.

Though celebrating peace with a cool head isn't flamboyant
as memorializing battles of bombs and bloodshed

I sing this song to the muse of peace, offer her
this my heart-tendered bouquet of flowers.

Apprehension

The tortoise taunts the tar doll with insults
the tar doll apprehends the talker with silence

O Aridon, take away the brassy rattle from me
but leave me the indestructible bronze of Benin

the fire-spitting fighter's consumed by his flames
take away the smoke and leave me unstoppable fire

I muffle my voice in the city of prattlers and gossips
let me be tongue-tied where free speech is let loose

I throw my phallus to the hyenas to be a new man
since wife-beaters justify savagery with body parts

I sire a clan of adorable children without lovemaking
I know the whole world without leaving my room

the antelope is not a drum but none without its death
martyr the antelope to transmit codes in the land of spirits

the cobra does not bite or swell to deter molestation
but who's so brave he dares catch it with bare hands?

Aridon, let my eloquence not come through a loud mouth
let my entire body not only speak for but also lead me

the festival is over another cycle will culminate in the next
the falcon disappears but won't fail to announce another year

the tortoise taunts the tar doll with insults
the tar doll apprehends the talker with silence.

We have grown

We have grown mature in our relationship;
I no longer promise you so many things,

things only heaven boasts of having in abundance
but globalization makes available in New York or Paris.

There have been thunderstorms despite the clear weather
I forecast; the Delta is much alive with unpredictability.

We have grown mature in the five years
we fooled ourselves with frank confessions

not knowing there's romance in the unknown
that will make us discoverers in the other's planet.

Don't mind the lessons of the more you know
the easier to put out fires we set upon ourselves!

We have grown mature in the relationship;
the mouse-and-cat understood as a friendly game.

We now repeat ourselves knowing call-and-response
does not make music monotonous but rhythmical.

We are still more than a hundred miles away
to the promised land of our first vows—

distance and proximity have embroiled us in
forgetfulness—embodied or disembodied,

we are never far from each other in the interstices
of the globe where we live at opposite ends.

We have matured in the relationship;
careful youth has turned us into reckless adults—

why will the cock and hen not abandon themselves
to dance into each other now they fear no hawks?

We have grown in the relationship,
knowing every question doesn't need a yes or a no—

we can be wrong and at the same time right
condemned and acquitted for love by the same jury;

we provide prosecutors and defenders from the same
jury of sentimental peers, one judge two different robes.

We have grown mature in the relationship;
you are no longer disappointed in me

and I don't cherish expectations of too much;
hence we are plodding closer to the destination

we set ourselves thinking of flying where love
sets its forlorn goal. Everywhere isn't easy to reach.

For Ayesiri

(after the Vietnamese *lu-shih*)

1

You didn't keep me out in the cold.
You opened the door despite reservation.

A homeless man suffers the bite of neglect—
the harmattan makes no friends with farmers.

Many will not experience this warmth of a hearth
in a hundred years of chasing dreams under wicked blasts.

Because of you I feel fortunate, a favorite
of God to be so loved in an accursed season.

2

Why did God make the flower so beautiful
but banned eyes from ever resting on it?

Why endow a fruit with heavenly sweetness
and forbid desirous mouths from tasting it?

Everybody is a thief until caught in the act
by those who are also thieves at heart.

I'll do all it takes to tend my fragrant garden.
Intense hunger absolves one from normal restraint.

3

Ask me the same question you would the moon—
why change so often, now slim soon full; clear and dark?

Ask the same question you would the sun—
why so restless you are daily on your feet?

I have the mouth of a mountain full of echoes.
I am the underground river you cross without a boat.

When you appeared divinely untouchable, I hugged you.
When I grew furs to cover roughness, you cuddled me.

Pantun* suite

1

Through a crack of the prison wall
come loud shouts for freedom—
the famished flower plant remembers
the rain and soil of the blooming season.

2

The text message evades the security cordon;
deleted as soon as digested before inspection—
denials can no longer be absolute;
the sun rises and sets over night's dominion.

3

The mask maintains its legendary silence,
except for esoteric chants that amplify its mystique—
the spirit speaks not but the body's talkative.
Without effort the wiregrass dances in the wind.

---

* pantun: an indigenous Malaysian poetic form.

(Re)visitation

It takes time but a (re)visitation will take place
when one incident holds another to the mirror.

Forty years ago I saw an Ojojo schoolgirl
give her recess rice money to a beggar;

one smeared by others' inhuman disgust
received a smile and cash that cheered him.

One that adults and rich made subhuman
by turning away from rather than confront

as the wreck of their species that needs
to be redeemed through collective effort!

And that's the visitation that came after so
many years have passed but never too late

as today I see several beggars pans in hand.
I remember her who truly loved and lived it—

I learned a lifetime's lesson on a Warri street,
knowing what to do as others pass them by.

Homage: To my friend's father

The fugitive takes every road that opens to him
even if he has to run through thorns and briars
or cross rivers with available craft to ferry him
rather than hit a fence and wait to be picked
and returned to chattel labor from dawn to dusk.
That was your father's fate after tasting raw
the sour diet of a polygamous household, after
his mother could not cope and quit the marriage,
leaving him to the legendary tyranny of stepmothers
and a father whose remaining wives held him hostage
in his own dominion after draining him dry of
everything that once made him man and master.
And he who flees death in an open road runs fast,
farther and farther to witness dawn in another land
whose daily calendar is not marked with whiplashes
or hunger; a new home whose tasks do not stifle.
It was at the market where living and dead consort
under cover of crowds and anonymity that the flight
in the freedom lane began to escape instant pursuit.
He arrived at Onitsha as ward of his maternal uncle
and there, in place of selling palm oil for his father,
with his maternal family name entered school where
he outshone most students to qualify for university
and would rise by industry to be a general manager.
In-between, by arrangement, he married your mom;
coming second you bore your grandfather's name—
rather than continue denying the family's crooked roots,
he chose to confront and break the jinx of uncaring fathers.
Knowing the love he had been denied as a child, he so
treated his favorite and other kids to biscuits and cakes
that today words as warm as a newly baked loaf tell

contentment of kids and the daughter's sweet tooth.
Freedom is the goal of fugitives; solace to whoever
throws off a stifling cloak to breathe free, live free.

Death of a senator

1

Here premonitions stalk every fatality
as happened before the senator's passing:

bees clustered his townhome and, chased away
with fire, next day congregated in his Abuja home.

The illiterate folks read the signs clearly;
only the blind see nothing ahead of them

and in the land of spirits no blind seeking
refuge from what they can't see after them.

With billions stacked in empty rooms,
spirits barrage the owner for the booty;

always on his feet on the floor the senator
draws firepower of archers tired of oration.

And so to ambition be the blame or glory—
for one short to aim at rising to the sun,

for one to dream stepping out of the senate
into the executive throne of a state chieftain

inflames the spleen of spirit head hunters
to put everyone alive on his rightful place.

Every caucus has become a coven and there
a simple handshake strips one of fortifications

for death the great masquerade to come robed
in stroke and fatigue, fabrics of strange sources

to silence the vociferous one always on his feet.
Mortality inflicted by spirits that cannot be tried.

2

Doubters and believers mourn the fall;
another calamity graces the morbid land

too uninhabitable, too vicious the same land
of parties for the dead and meaningless titles.

"They have struck again; they never
leave alone our great ones!" one cried.

"He didn't help his relatives," they chorus
in his mansion where he used to fete them.

"He was too ambitious. Why never satisfied?"
say colleagues who had applauded his rhetoric.

Before the interment, the colleagues begin
to fight for the vacated money-doubling seat

and boast in orgies of senator-in-waiting;
they sow fire seeds for wandering spirits.

So spirits stampede everywhere with pitfalls
and to great ambition be the blame or glory

for the world cannot speak with one voice.
Whose dish can satisfy every appetite?

And the seeing watch spirits in festive fashion
celebrate their morbid fortune at his funeral.

Let them die for Arsenal

"I am ready to die for Arsenal" (Nigerian fan as Arsenal played Hull City on May 17, 2014 in the days of *Bringbackourgirls*)

Let them die for Arsenal
and millions more for Chelsea, Manchu, and Real Madrid
those who hide as neighbors die from armed robbery
those who do nothing seeing their property carted away
those who watch their mothers, wives, and daughters raped
those who pay phantom light bills for blackout months
those whose reps steal their share of the national wealth
those who abandon their children in war to save themselves
those who flee rather than club to death the cobra at the doorstep.

Let them die for Arsenal
those who raise not arms against brutish police and soldiers
those who choose to accept kola rather than simple truth
those who "hammer" rather than live on honest hard work
those who stop not after a perilous pothole to plant a red flag
those who refuse to be eyes of the blind and feet of the crippled
those who sell body parts to build mansions they won't live in
those defecating daily on their parents' forgotten graves
those who abandon fellow travelers involved in ghastly accidents.

Let them die for Arsenal
die for Arsenal, die for all the Europa clubs
and let the strong breed here live on
die for Arsenal and rid the land of a contagion
die for Arsenal and rid the land of psychos and suicides
die for Arsenal, die for Chelsea and avert a national implosion
die for Arsenal, die for Manchu and rid the streets of loose cannons
die for Arsenal, die for Real Madrid and rid the neighborhood of rot

die for Arsenal, die for Ajax and rid the state of fifth columnists.

Let them die for Arsenal
die for a white-robed masquerade
die for a tall hat trick
die for the golden rule of sudden death
die for a stealth hard shot
die for a coconut header
die for an assist ball
die for dirty passes
die for hitting the ball hard.

Die for Arsenal
die not from Holy Ghost fire
die not from the menace of witchcraft
die not from kicking an empty bucket
die not from a poisonous snakebite
die not from a motor crash
die not from defending the handicapped against abusers
die not from a massive heart attack
die, die, die for Arsenal.

You don't die for many causes
you don't die for Arsenal and still die for Nigeria
you die for only one cause
you don't die for Arsenal and still bring back our stolen children
there's only one death
die for Arsenal and you are gone as a person
you have only one life
throw it away for Arsenal and desecrate your homeland
die for Arsenal.

Die for Arsenal, my king of fools
die for Arsenal, my retarded brother
die for Arsenal, my homeless relative
die for Arsenal whose body will be carcass for vultures

die for Arsenal, whose body won't be buried in England
die for Arsenal, stray rabid dog
die for Arsenal, my compatriot
die for Arsenal who will not die for God
let them all die for Arsenal.

In a tent room

(at Kilifi, Coastal Kenya)

In a tent room
in the savannah

the beautiful landscape
Umoja and Jambo

lions and zealots roam
none saner than the other

I think of the lady in Teotihuacan
before the Moon and Sun

without words giving me
a bear hug to share love of her race

Senegalese traders smiling to me
in the nether world of Frisian Holland

migrant workers speaking Bini
complaining to me in Almeria

in Edinburgh an old lady needing
my attention calling out Jimmy.

In a tent room
a beach front of the savannah

so many memories assault me
not to forget the beauty I have seen

and yet so imperiled, the sun rising
amidst waves carrying odds and ends

from underworld depths; they still live
despite being buried for centuries.

Masks

We deck our walls with masks
our gods imprisoned in wood or terracotta

we deck our walls with godly faces
of youth and beauty

we recover our losses in masked figures
we regain permanence in bodies of masks

rather than disintegrate with the homes we live in
but on the walls of daily existence hang the masks

the godly beauty of long ago bristling in youth
we want to hold to life for as long as it takes

we can't forsake the mask though the shrine
no longer the convocation ground of spirits

the mask hangs above our heads on the wall
where lit the eyes see it with deserving awe

the gods have left us with masks they blessed
to sell their stories and sing their songs

they show the beauty that does not fade
the masks remind us of what not to forget

despite the mold of abandoned shrines everywhere
hold to the lives of gods slipping from our hands

what we cannot carry we nail tight to the wall
the mask is a mirror of beauty of the ageless

the pantheon of gods breathe loud in the masks
that deck my walls with somber remembrances

the gods have abandoned their shrines, wandering
in the void that worshipers create out of desolation

conversions made of cowries into dollars
folks abandon their gods not to talk of leaders

I cheer myself that I am still young at sixty-five
now a mask on the wall nailed to outlast the home

abandoned the gods of yesteryears the masks
hanging on walls of bungalows and apartments

I see the masks on the wall relive my great boys
I was once a god sauntering to cover the land

my mask freezes a wild smile or childish grin
and on the wall the body keeps faith with gods

I was such a sensational figure before graying hair.
I used to be a god now a mask on the painted wall!

Wrestlers

(after Bruce Onobrakpeya's painting of that name)

It's not only the brawny muscled that are paired
in a wrestling match; nor hulk against lazybones—

such contests easily come to a conclusion
but not when two feeble hands lock in combat.

And there stood two on the *erierie* tender grass
that would not sway because of their lightweight!

Each skeletal and skimmed of fat to defy gravity,
a pin head and long crooked sticks for legs and arms

borne by weightless grass suspended in the air
with a décor of green cocoyam leaves floating.

Who would doubt the evenness of their measurement;
who would bet on either of the two as lazier of the lazy?

So the epic duel of the lightest of lazybones continued
day after day until three years passed without a victor—

neither the stem of grass nor its multiple branches
swayed because of the two weightless contestants;

neither rain nor sunshine helped one against the other.
No weather made firmer the foothold or caused a slip;

daylight exposed no weakness that one seized upon.
Night gave none the craft to steal upon the other's heels;

there was no energy whether cheered by a crowd
or met by silence—no advantage to either wrestler.

When the king of the lazy intervened to stop the fight,
he slipped, knocked head against a cocoyam leaf and died.

Only the death of their king stopped the unending duel
but none cared because a peace maker died for them!

Of humidity and hydration

"This sun go make man crazy" (Warri madman)

1

This sun will surely drive someone crazy.
It breathes fire with the vengeance of a hurt god.

The sun is at its meanest when not saturated,
it is up to the chin in hell and so unforgiving;

the sun is my neighbor the same sun my boss
it suffers the indignity of a scorned spouse on heat.

It heeds nobody's entreaties for forgiveness,
the sun is a cultic god and better beg it not for favor;

the sun is the nation's president the *oga* at the top,
it lives in Aso Rock in a planet beyond reach.

There's no way of predicting its mood this season,
breathing fire it breeds tears and owes no apologies;

the earth may be warming up but the sun has fixed ways,
the president keeps distant till electioneering campaigns.

The sun suffers no qualms for those afflicted with burns,
the troubled palace envied from afar as only carousing.

The sun sleeps not daily in traversing the earth nonstop
and so suffers from chronic insomnia as curse of godhead;

the sun suffers headaches and all forms of addiction,
it drinks and yet thirsty it smokes but remains excitable.

The sun is fond of frivolities strips beauties naked;
the sun salivates from obscene spectacles before it.

It turns the heat on those who worship it without hearts,
it blackmails the moon from parading its starry maidens.

The sun will surely drive someone crazy like a madman
in the open roasting bread for corn, boiling Coke to make tea!

2

The proximity of the river didn't douse the homes aflame:
the sun shot flares into every direction and burned the skin,

the abundance of oil brought no respite from blackouts
as the wealth of the nation no relief from lacerating misery.

The church erected no cast wall bulwark against corruption
and pastors and congregations lost to God's malevolent rival

to toy with as cannons shot into space without expectation
of a return or soft-landing in the vast abyss of nothingness.

There's humidity of the soil, humidity of the body as well
as the intolerable humidity of the nation and commonwealth—

there's no succor to the humidity which the equator suffers;
the equator is a vast state whose president sweats profusely.

I cannot pick the ripe fruits in the forest by exclusion of age
but I see poachers wage war against the arboreal population;

the forest sweats from flares the rivers sweat from spills
the game life trapped beyond the basic rules of survival.

Blame the humidity on the sun washing your view away,
blame the humidity on brains that refused to be resourceful.

My country is an arthritic nation with all the resources
but disabled in ways too daunting to spring out of damnation—

blame it on humidity for not tapping sense out of big brains;
blame Providence for giving wealth to who cannot manage it!

The sun has tagged a nation for unrelenting fire-power;
the sun demands a ransom on the carousers in Abuja—

if a foreign nincompoop had this much, imagine the results
like a pauper daydreaming he had Dangote's wealth; imagine!

Next to God

"When in pain, next to God is the doctor" (Tijan M. Sallah)

When a patient next to God is the doctor
when a student next to God is the professor
when a sportsman next to God is the coach
when a farmer next to God is the weatherman
when a lover next to God is the beloved
when a minstrel next to God is the muse

because

God is the doctor prescribing medicines for a cure
God is the professor dispensing knowledge from a fountain
God is the coach who writes the victory playbook
God is the weatherman forecasting a record harvest
God is the beloved healing the lacerated heart
God is the muse whose memory is a storehouse of tales

and

He heals in answer to prayers
He provides knowledge from inexhaustible sources
He exhorts towards victory
He fills the crops with miracle nutrients
He provides the uplifting smile
He releases a stream of superhuman songs.

Waiting

("for a river waits for the fisherman"—Dike Okoro)

The river waits for the fisherman
the forest waits for the hunter

the land waits for the farmer
the deity waits for devotees

the office waits for its workers
dawn waits for the cockerel's call

the market waits for sellers and buyers
the road waits for travelers

the year waits for months to pass
the egg waits to hatch a new life

the sea waits for the river's tribute
the earth waits to swallow every birth

there's always one waiting for the other
and eventually an end to every journey.

For the New Year

The year ends; it begins not in youth.
The year begins; it ends not in age.

The heralding of another season comes
with the reality of cold or hot, wet or dry—

every beginning grows out of something giving way
while every ending longs for a fresh start.

A new day runs inexorably with the sun
two partners through a course of familiarity;

they go under cover of light but often
complete their task in the dark of sleep.

I have amassed old and new resources
to cope with life that thrives on escaping death;

it's not the seasons that bring freshness to us
variegated costumes we are compelled to endure

but the routine that's neither new nor old,
strangers more at home than you would admit.

And that's the love I seek: what neither begins
with promise of age nor ends in its youth.

As the year ends, I hear songs of life reiterate
tunes I have heard daily serenade me and others;

as the New Year comes to view, I am dressed in costumes
it has gathered to come with seasons of remembrance and hope;

two messengers that proffer me gifts I tuck away.
My life mends old into new, wearing the fashionable.

Another year will begin; this is ending not because of age.
The New Year will gather dust; it begins with resolutions,

stacks of wishes being deployed with fanfare into the future
from the dissipated abundance of what we fritter and remember.

At the journey's end for sure we are at the starting point
poised as ever to remember the hope that bestirs us

from losing what we wish ourselves but can't grasp—
the New Year coming and going, neither young nor old.

Kraftgriots

Also in the series (POETRY) *continued*

Ebi Yeibo: *Maiden Lines* (2004)
Barine Ngaage: *Rhythms of Crisis* (2004)
Funso Aiyejina: *I, The Supreme & Other Poems* (2004)
'Lere Oladitan: *Boolekaja: Lagos Poems 1* (2005)
Seyi Adigun: *Bard on the Shore* (2005)
Famous Dakolo: *A Letter to Flora* (2005)
Olawale Durojaiye: *An African Night* (2005)
G. 'Ebinyo Ogbowei: *let the honey run & other poems* (2005)
Joe Ushie: *Popular Stand & Other Poems* (2005)
Gbemisola Adeoti: *Naked Soles* (2005)
Aj. Dagga Tolar: *This Country is not a Poem* (2005)
Tunde Adeniran: *Labyrinthine Ways* (2006)
Sophia Obi: *Tears in a Basket* (2006)
Tonyo Biriabebe: *Undercurrents* (2006)
Ademola O. Dasylva: *Songs of Odamolugbe* (2006), winner, 2006 ANA/Cadbury poetry prize
George Ehusani: *Flames of Truth* (2006)
Abubakar Gimba: *This Land of Ours* (2006)
G. 'Ebinyo Ogbowei: *the heedless ballot box* (2006)
Hyginus Ekwuazi: *Love Apart* (2006), winner, 2007 ANA/NDDC Gabriel Okara poetry prize and winner, 2007 ANA/Cadbury poetry prize
Abubakar Gimba: *Inner Rumblings* (2006)
Albert Otto: *Letters from the Earth* (2007)
Aj. Dagga Tolar: *Darkwaters Drunkard* (2007)
Idris Okpanachi: *The Eaters of the Living* (2007), winner, 2008 ANA/Cadbury poetry prize
Tubal-Cain: *Mystery in Our Stream* (2007), winner, 2006 ANA/NDDC Gabriel Okara poetry prize
John Iwuh: *Ashes & Daydreams* (2007)
Sola Owonibi: *Chants to the Ancestors* (2007)
Adewale Aderinale: *The Authentic* (2007)
Ebi Yeibo: *The Forbidden Tongue* (2007)
Doutimi Kpakiama: *Salute to our Mangrove Giants* (2008)
Halima M. Usman: *Spellbound* (2008)
Hyginus Ekwuazi: *Dawn Into Moonlight: All Around Me Dawning* (2008), winner, 2008 ANA/NDDC Gabriel Okara poetry prize
Ismail Bala Garba & Abdullahi Ismaila (eds.): *Pyramids: An Anthology of Poems from Northern Nigeria* (2008)
Denja Abdullahi: *Abuja Nunyi (This is Abuja)* (2008)
Japhet Adeneye: *Poems for Teenagers* (2008)
Seyi Hodonu: *A Tale of Two in Time (Letters to Susan)* (2008)

Ibukun Babarinde: *Running Splash of Rust and Gold* (2008)
Chris Ngozi Nkoro: *Trails of a Distance* (2008)
Tunde Adeniran: *Beyond Finalities* (2008)
Abba Abdulkareem: *A Bard's Balderdash* (2008)
Ifeanyi D. Ogbonnaya: *... And Pigs Shall Become House Cleaners* (2008)
g'ebinyõ ogbowei: *the town crier's song* (2009)
g'ebinyõ ogbowei: *song of a dying river* (2009)
Sophia Obi-Apoko: *Floating Snags* (2009)
Akachi Adimora-Ezeigbo: *Heart Songs* (2009), winner, 2009 ANA/Cadbury poetry prize
Hyginus Ekwuazi: *The Monkey's Eyes* (2009)
Seyi Adigun: *Prayer for the Mwalimu* (2009)
Faith A. Brown: *Endless Season* (2009)
B.M. Dzukogi: *Midnight Lamp* (2009)
B.M. Dzukogi: *These Last Tears* (2009)
Chimezie Ezechukwu: *The Nightingale* (2009)
Ummi Kaltume Abdullahi: *Tiny Fingers* (2009)
Ismaila Bala & Ahmed Maiwada (eds.): *Fireflies: An Anthology of New Nigerian Poetry* (2009)
Eugenia Abu: *Don't Look at Me Like That* (2009)
Data Osa Don-Pedro: *You Are Gold and Other Poems* (2009)
Sam Omatseye: *Mandela's Bones and Other Poems* (2009)
Sam Omatseye: *Dear Baby Ramatu* (2009)
C.O. Iyimoga: *Fragments in the Air* (2010)
Bose Ayeni-Tsevende: *Streams* (2010)
Seyi Hodonu: *Songs from My Mother's Heart (2010),* winner ANA/NDDC Gabriel Okara poetry prize, 2010
Akachi Adimora-Ezeigbo: *Waiting for Dawn* (2010)
Hyginus Ekwuazi: *That Other Country* (2010), winner, ANA/Cadbury poetry prize, 2010
Emmanuel Frank-Opigo: *Masks and Facades* (2010)
Tosin Otitoju: *Comrade* (2010)
Arnold Udoka: *Poems Across Borders* (2010)
Arnold Udoka: *The Gods Are So Silent & Other Poems* (2010)
Abubakar Othman: *The Passions of Cupid* (2010)
Okinba Launko: *Dream-Seeker on Divining Chain* (2010)
'kufre ekanem: *the ant eaters* (2010)
McNezer Fasehun: *Ever Had a Dear Sister* (2010)
Baba S. Umar: *A Portrait of My People* (2010)
Gimba Kakanda: *Safari Pants* (2010)
Sam Omatseye: *Lion Wind & Other Poems* (2011)
Ify Omalicha: *Now that Dreams are Born* (2011)
Karo Okokoh: *Souls of a Troubadour* (2011)
Ada Onyebuenyi, Chris Ngozi Nkoro, Ebere Chukwu (eds): *Uto Nka: An Anthology of Literature for Fresh Voices* (2011)
Mabel Osakwe: *Desert Songs of Bloom* (2011)

Pious Okoro: *Vultures of Fortune & Other Poems* (2011)
Godwin Yina: *Clouds of Sorrows* (2011)
Nnimmo Bassey: *I Will Not Dance to Your Beat* (2011)
Denja Abdullahi: *A Thousand Years of Thirst* (2011)
Enoch Ojotisa: *Commoner's Speech* (2011)
Rowland Timi Kpakiama: *Bees and Beetles* (2011)
Niyi Osundare: *Random Blues* (2011)
Lawrence Ogbo Ugwuanyi: *Let Them Not Run* (2011)
Saddiq M. Dzukogi: *Canvas* (2011
Arnold Udoka: *Running with My Rivers* (2011)
Olusanya Bamidele: *Erased Without a Trace* (2011)
Olufolake Jegede: *Treasure Pods* (2012)
Karo Okokoh: *Songs of a Griot* (2012), winner. ANA/NDDC Gabriel Okara poetry prize, 2012
Musa Idris Okpanachi: *From the Margins of Paradise* (2012)
John Martins Agba: *The Fiend and Other Poems* (2012)
Sunnie Ododo: *Broken Pitchers* (2012)
'Kunmi Adeoti: *Epileptic City* (2012)
Ibiwari Ikiriko: *Oily Tears of the Delta* (2012)
Bala Dalhatu: *Moonlights* (2012)
Karo Okokoh: *Manna for the Mind* (2012)
Chika O. Agbo: *The Fury of the Gods* (2012)
Emmanuel C. S. Ojukwu: *Beneath the Sagging Roof* (2012)
Amirikpa Oyigbenu: *Cascades and Flakes* (2012)
Ebi Yeibo: *Shadows of the Setting Sun* (2012)
Chikaoha Agoha: *Shreds of Thunder* (2012)
Mark Okorie: *Terror Verses* (2012)
Clemmy Igwebike-Ossi: *Daisies in the Desert* (2012)
Idris Amali: *Back Again (At the Foothills of Greed)* (2012)
A.N. Akwanya: *Visitant on Tiptoe* (2012)
Akachi Adimora-Ezeigbo: *Dancing Masks* (2013)
Chinazo-Bertrand Okeomah: *Furnace of Passion* (2013)
g'ebinyõ ogbowei: *marsh boy and other poems* (2013)
Ifeoma Chinwuba: *African Romance* (2013)
Remi Raji: *Sea of my Mind* (2013)
Francis Odinya: *Never Cry Again in Babylon* (2013)
Immanuel Unekwuojo Ogu: *Musings of a Pilgrim* (2013)
Khabyr Fasasi: *Tongues of Warning* (2013)
J.C.P. Christopher: *Salient Whispers* (2014)
Paul T. Liam: *Saint Sha'ade and other poems* (2014)
Joy Nwiyi: *Burning Bottom* (2014)
R. Adebayo Lawal: *Melodreams* (2014)
R. Adebayo Lawal: *Music of the Muezzin* (2014)
Idris Amali: *Efeega: War of Ants* (2014)
Samuel Onungwe: *Tantrums of a King* (2014)

Bizuum G. Yadok: *Echoes of the Plateau* (2014)
Abubakar Othman: *Bloodstreams in the Desert* (2014)
rome aboh: *A Torrent of Terror* (2014)
Udenta O. Udenta: *37 Seasons Before the Tornado* (2015)
Magnus Abraham-Dukuma: *Dreams from the Creek* (2015)
Christian Otobotekere: *A Sailor's Son* (2015)
Tanure Ojaide: *The Tale of the Harmattan* (2015)
Festus Okwekwe: *Our Mother is Not a Woman* (2015)
Tunde Adeniran: *Fate and Faith* (2015)
Khabyr Fasasi: *Spells of Solemn Songs* (2015)
Chris Anyokwu: *Naked Truth* (2015)
Zoya Jibodu: *Melodies of Love* (2015)

Printed in the United States
By Bookmasters